EVERYTHING FEELS RECENT WHEN YOU'RE FAR AWAY

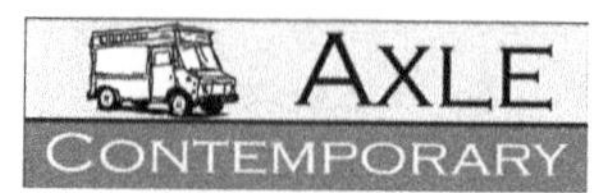

Published by Axle Contemporary
P.O. Box 22095
Santa Fe, New Mexico 87502
www.axlecontemporarypress.com

© 2021 Axle Contemporary. All rights reserved.

ISBN: 978-0-9963991-6-6

No part of the book may be used or reproduced without permission from the publisher.

All copyright for poems and artwork are retained by the individual writers and artists.

Cover drawing by Jessi Lopez.

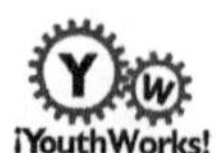
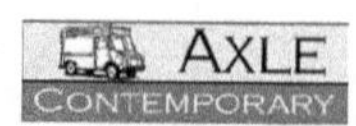
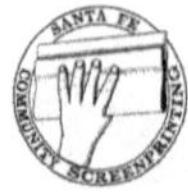

academy of
american poets

EVERYTHING FEELS RECENT WHEN YOU'RE FAR AWAY

POETRY AND ART FROM SANTA FE YOUTH
DURING THE PANDEMIC

I am entirely grateful to the Academy of American Poets for awarding a Poets Laureate Fellowship to me, which funded our civic project, including this anthology. I am equally thankful to the City of Santa Fe, Mayor Alan Webber and the Santa Fe Arts Commission for selecting me as the city's fifth Poet Laureate, and to the Witter Bynner Foundation for Poetry for their support of this position for our city. Matthew Chase-Daniel and Jerry Wellman of Axle Contemporary and I began to collaborate on this project— a poetry and visual art community celebration of and for our Santa Fe high school teenagers— before the onset of COVID-19. When I received the fellowship in April, 2020, the pandemic was full blown and we clearly had a lot of re-organizing to do, but our vision was large and each aspect of the project— the poetry workshops and poem writing, the T-shirt design, the T-shirt screenprinting, the photography and portrait making, the group shows and readings— was reconfigured. Applause for Zoom and the internet and technology for keeping us all together in its distinctive way during this time!

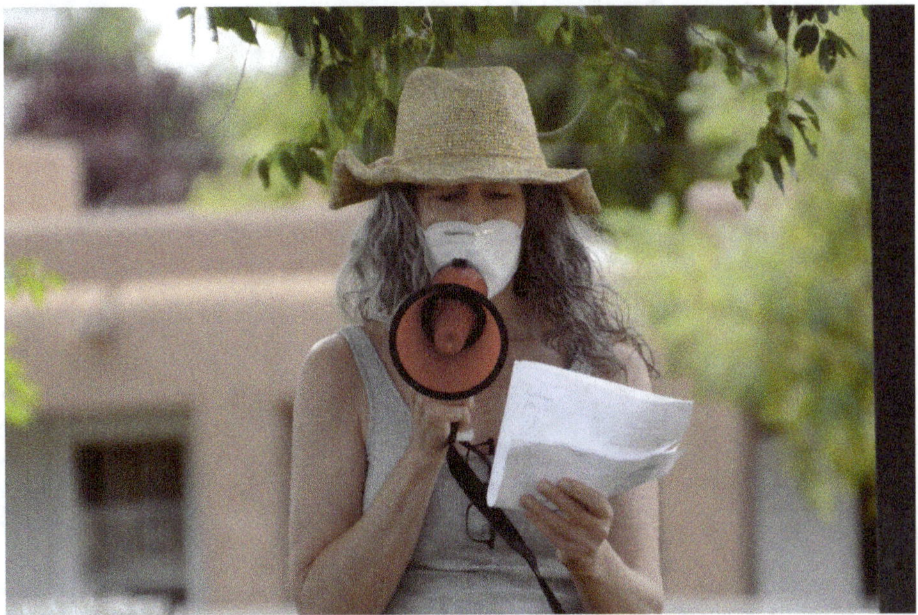

Our community partners shifted around as we continually updated what was available to us in light of Covid: I taught poetry classes in public parks and workshops on Zoom; Matthew and Jerry generated innovative videos and PDF in-depth instruction guides for t-shirt design and portraiture, enabling students to complete these phases at home; David Sloan from YouthWorks Screenprinting Studio generously printed all of the t-shirts himself as students could not visit the facility; the Railyard Performance Center donated their prominent railing in the bustling Railyard, an epicenter of the arts in Santa Fe, for a sizable installation of images and poems from the project; Collected Works Bookstore kindly offered to host our book launch and reading; and Axle Contemporary will present a Broadsides series on the exterior of the their Mobile Artspace in lieu of the show we had planned at the shuttered downtown Community Gallery.

While we were presented with unforeseen and unprecedented challenges throughout the span of this project, the perseverance, creativity and resilience of everyone involved sustained us, and in some ways, actually enhanced the project by affirming the significance of artistic expression to education and well-being. The fine work of the students speaks for itself. This project was for and about them; we are proud to have encouraged their imaginations and growth. *Everything Feels Recent When You're Far Away* is the penultimate line from Lesly Esparza's poem *Incense.* We chose this for the title of the anthology as the language not only elucidates a current state of presence during this pandemic, but is also prescient for what marvelously follows to end her poem: *Does an old thing know when a new thing will come?*

Elizabeth Jacobson
Santa Fe Poet Laureate
March 1, 2021

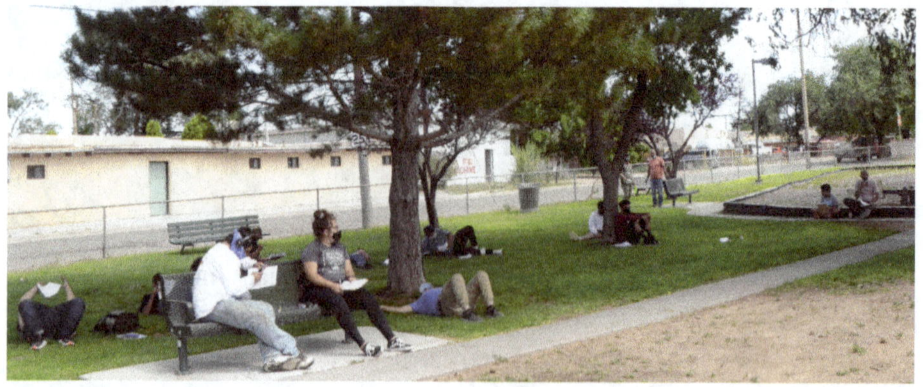

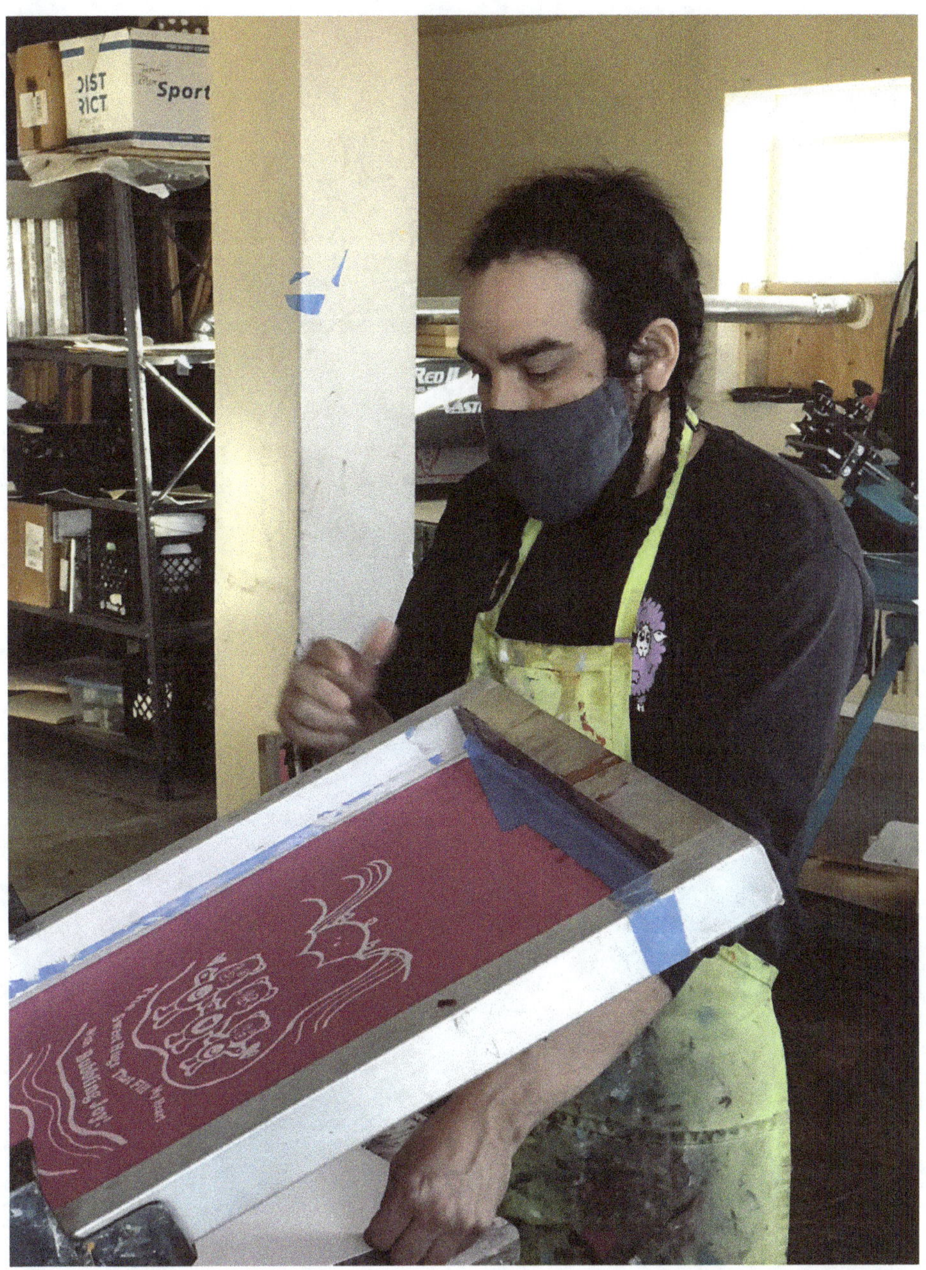

The Clock Strikes

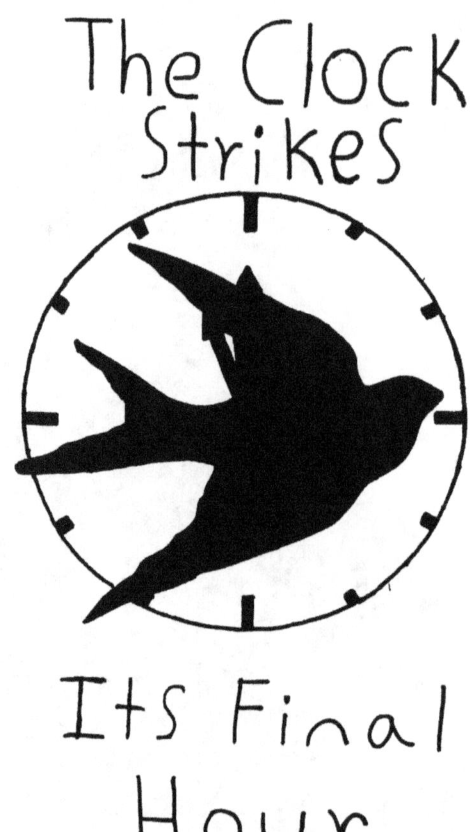

Its Final Hour

Jessi Lopez

Blackbird

The clock strikes
its final hour
it is here.
It's unfair
I did everything I was supposed to.

Sorrow fills inside me
as the cage opens.
A single black bird pokes its head out
from it's metal prison.
I stand a short distance away from it
looking into those merciless eyes.

I have cheated death
in my life times,
but
there's no more second chances.
This is my final chapter

arms wide open,
a desperate painful scream.
The black bird soaring through me,
taking my soul with it.

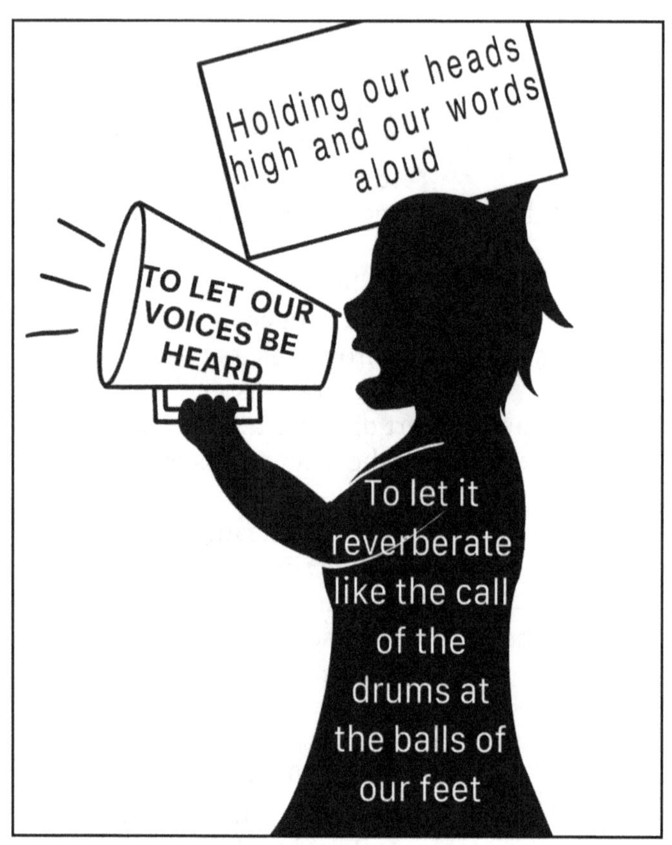

Sarita Sol Gonzalez

Voice

We weren't seen as enough
The world we lived in didn't see us as more than machines
to pump out men
Each daughter a maid
Each woman a wife
We were never willfully given the right to vote
Those who held more melanin on their wrists
had to work twice as hard than their sisters of fairer complexions
We thought we had all won the battle when we heard the celebration
But we quickly realized this victory was not for us all
Women of color still had to endure for 42 more years
Of being silenced
Holding our heads high and our words aloud
To let our voices be heard
To let it reverberate in their head like
The call of the drum at the balls of our feet
They say the fight ended in 1920
It is 2020
And the fight is not over
For a century we have fought for respect
Striving to survive in a world made for men
We still fight for equal pay
We still fight for our personal autonomy
We still fight for equality
We still fight for our voices to be heard
We still fight

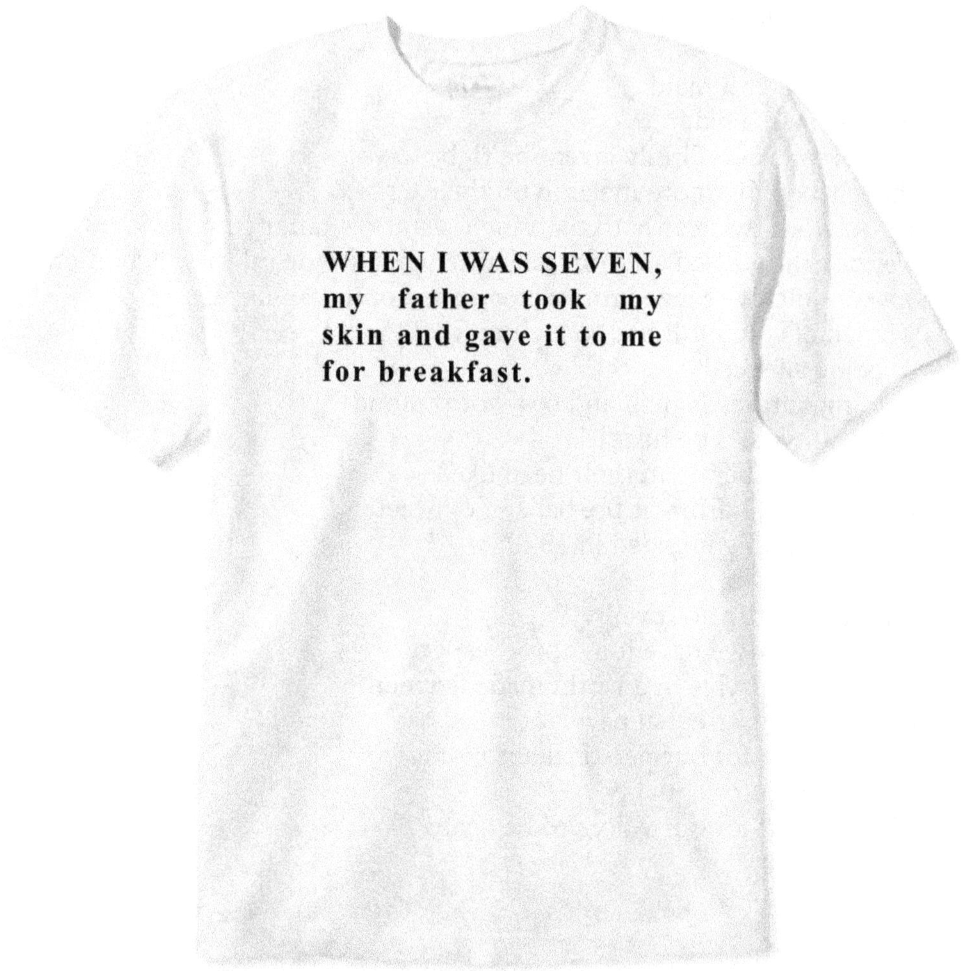

WHEN I WAS SEVEN,
my father took my
skin and gave it to me
for breakfast.

Dante Begay

MARION CRANE

WHEN I WAS SEVEN, my father took my skin and gave it to me for breakfast.

WHEN I WAS EIGHT, he took my bed and told me of Mary's crimes.

WHEN I WAS NINE, he took my eyes for garnish and sang me happy birthday.

WHEN I WAS TEN, he took the silver caps under my pillow.

WHEN I WAS TWELVE, he took the fireplace, brick by brick.

WHEN I WAS THIRTEEN, he took the folds of my brain.

WHEN I WAS FOURTEEN, he took the blood from my hymen.

I AM FIFTEEN, and he is taking the wires of my braces.

WHEN I AM SIXTEEN, he will take the doorhandles.

WHEN I AM SEVENTEEN, he will take my boyfriend's corsage.

WHEN I AM EIGHTEEN, he will take the vowels of my name.

WHEN I AM NINETEEN, he will take his wife back.

I AM SEVEN when I take his silver band and melt it for scrap.

I AM EIGHT when I take his teeth and scatter them across the desert.

I AM NINE when I take his badge and brand his neck.

I AM TEN when I take his wife and hang her with her veil.

I AM ELEVEN when I take the hubcaps of his Camaro.

I AM TWELVE when I take his fists and feed them to the junkyard dogs.

I AM THIRTEEN when I take his shoes and throw them over the power line.

I AM FOURTEEN when I take his pockets and fill them with boulders.

I AM FIFTEEN, and I am going to take his guitar strings and suffocate him.

WHEN I AM SIXTEEN, I am going to take his head and hear the maggots decline the meal.

WHEN I AM SEVENTEEN, I am going to take his feet and use them as wedding gifts.

WHEN I AM EIGHTEEN, I am going to take his rosary and leave it at a yard sale.

WHEN I AM NINETEEN, I am going to take his son and return his ears.

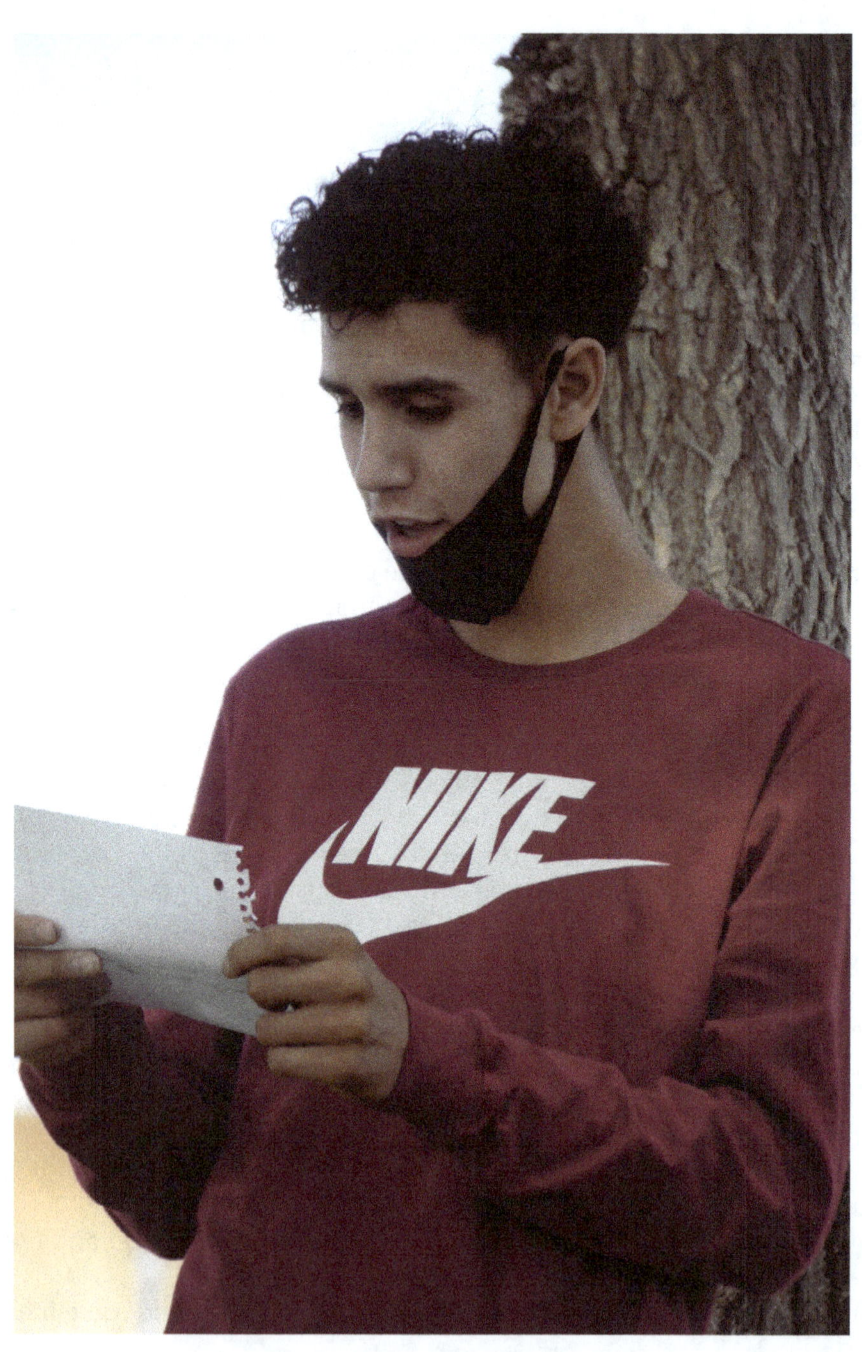
NIKE

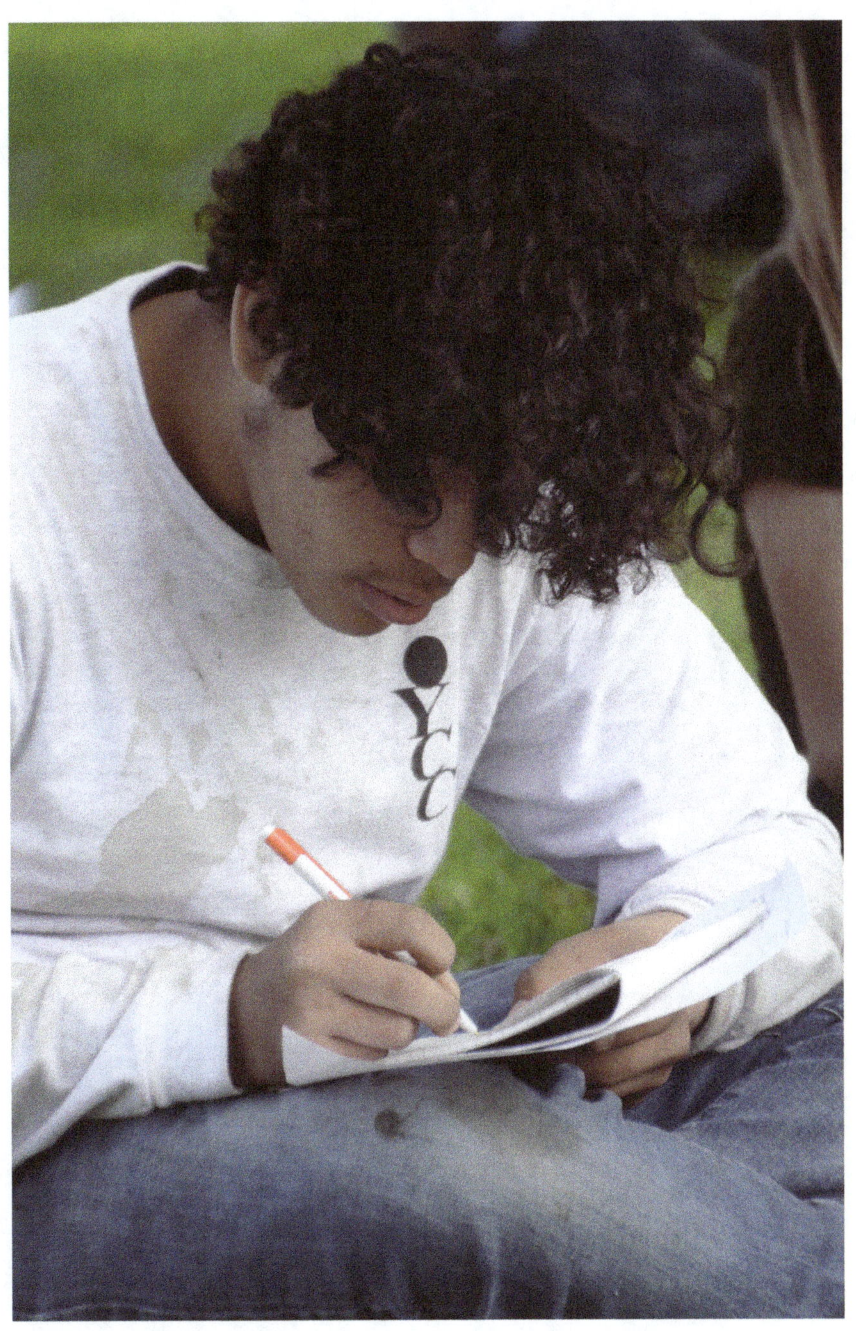

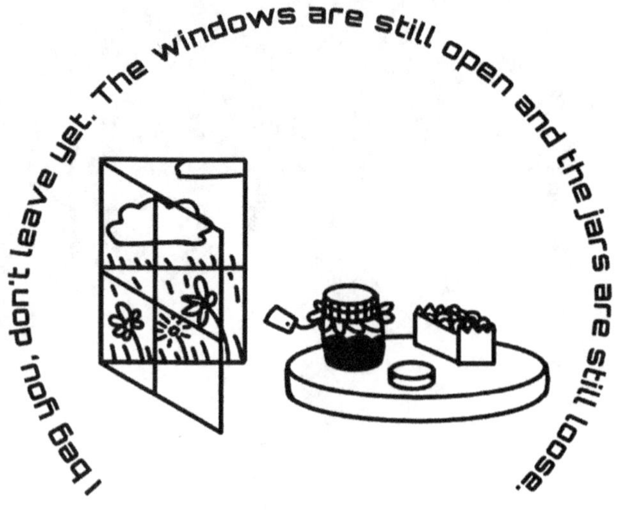

Tiana Padilla

Who are you if not the detached unawareness
of my deepest muscle memories?
I beg you, don't leave yet, the windows are still open
And the jars are still loose
How much do you remember?
In my constant desperation to keep you near
I'll gladly fill in the gaps for you

How much do I have left this week?

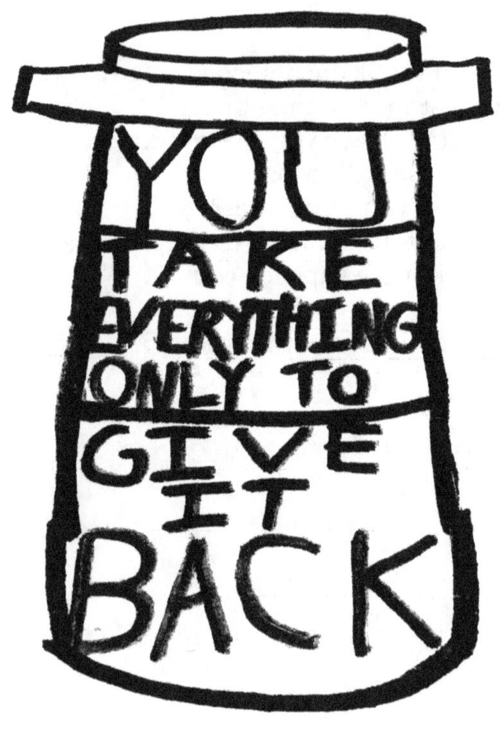

Alejandro Partida

Entertain

You give me so much to do,
yet at the same time nothing.
You take everything,
only to give it back.

You are the ghost
that will fix me forever.
You are the worry,
that I will always have on my mind

You only entertain.
Only entertain.
To me you are an old flame,
that always comes back for more.

I ask myself,
every single day.
Why do you satisfy me?

I always say I'll stop,
yet I never do.
I know that it's not alright,
Yet there is no turning back

You only entertain.
Only entertain.
I always feel so much shame,
I feel I am at war

Should I have just one or should I take two,
what am I becoming.
You're something I keep burying,
please just cut me some slack.

I regret you the most,
you're my worst endeavour.
I must hurry,
to get you out of my mind.

Why do you entertain?
How do you entertain?

You give me so much to do, and nothing
You take everything, only
to give it back.

You are the ghost that will fix me, forever.
You worry my mind, always.
You entertain.

You only entertain, old flame, you
Always come back for more.
Why do you satisfy?

I'll stop.
I never do.
It's not right.
Turning back?

You only entertain.
Only entertain
To entertain

So much shame,
I feel I am at war
Only to entertain.

Should I have just one or take two?
What am I becoming? You're something
I keep burying

Regret, my worst endeavour.
I must rush to get you out
of my mind.

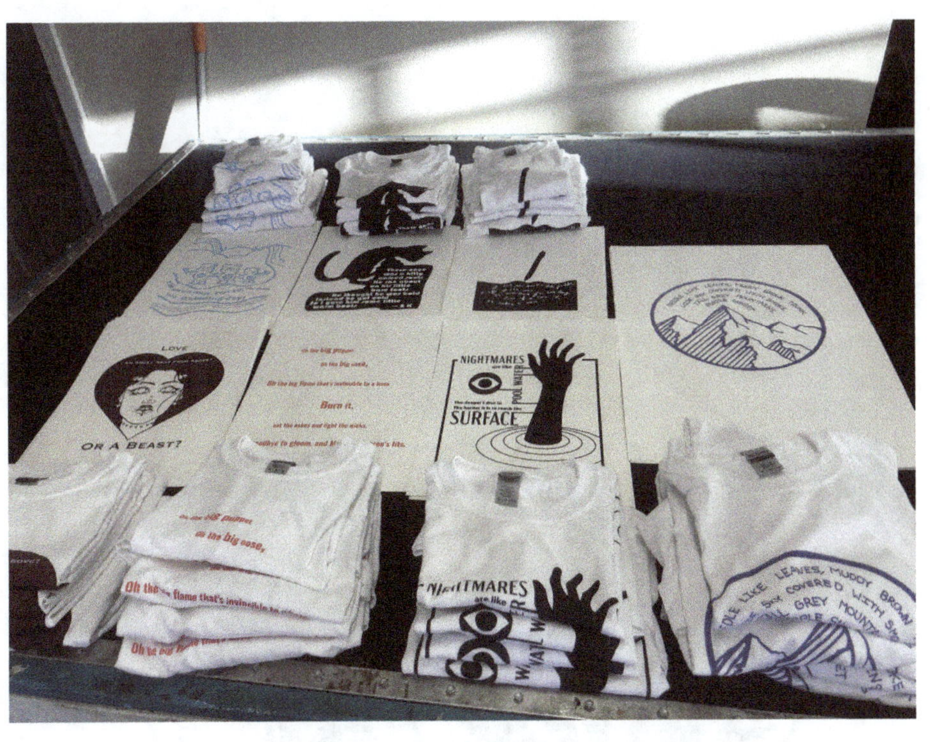

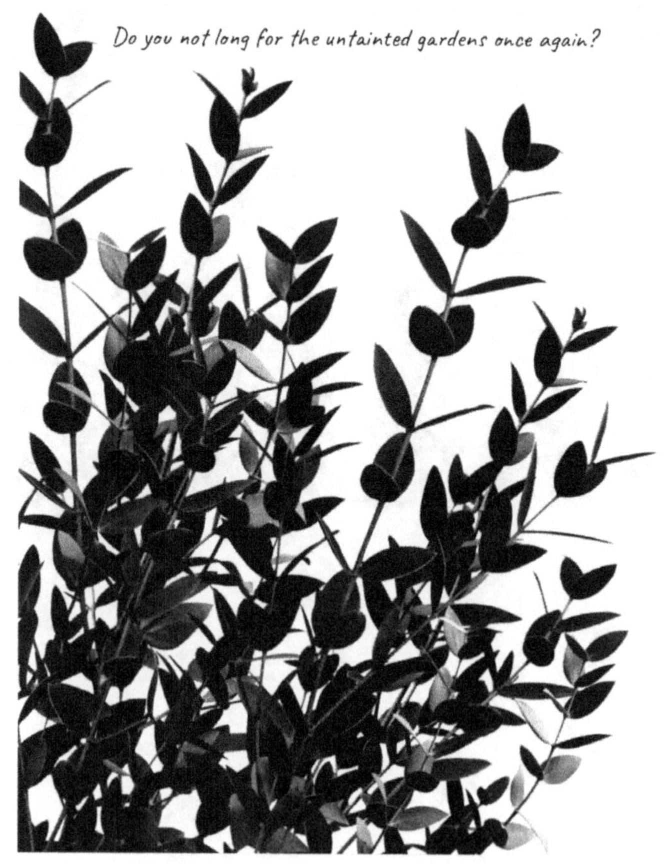

Serenity Castor

So We Lie In A Poppy Field, Unbeknownst

Sweet girl, let me place a kiss on your head while
One by one, the savory, nourished apples are bitten.
Selfishly and carelessly, we watch, and
They bite.

Strange, albeit familiar,
I aim to shield you, and yet
Nails mark palms to keep sane.

It's silly, but I pray.
Do you not long for the untainted gardens once again?
I pray.

May evil never be graced by your eyes, girl.
And I pray,
The apple now tastes bitter.

Sweet girl,
Forced to see all,
Do you long for the chance to disappear?

A palm to a fist, to the air, to a bitter string of shaky shouts.
Sweet girl, there are too many serpents to bear.
I contend, I confess, will you ever forgive?

The world is now left bare, and
I long to take you to the garden forevermore, where
Open fields will roll out before us, grass looming over bugs

The clouds will prance in their orange hued sky
And at last, we will lay
Lay in a field of poppies, unbeknownst

Every piece of concrete,
powdered; dusted into a
crackling of white noise,
So poised you are, white
noise . . . .

Maia Hillock-Katz

Ode to The Breeze

I cannot lie here without thinking.
How you carry every thought away
Every piece of concrete, powdered;
Dusted into a crackling of white noise,
So poised you are, white noise

I cannot lie here without noticing.
How you knock on the doors of hope,
Using your cleansing powers of serene soap
Bubbles over my thoughts
as you wash

I cannot lie here without gratitude.
How you rassle the tree's leaves,
Dance between the caverns,
Lace your steps between the blades of grass,
So light, as you play, like dusted brass

So when the blistering thoughts bubble over
And I am just left with fog and
The walls of my mind expand; me
The size of an ant, you,
You blow the fog away

So when the drawstrings of the hoodie
don't cinch tight enough
And I can't curl small enough
You, you blow the drawstrings away
So poised.

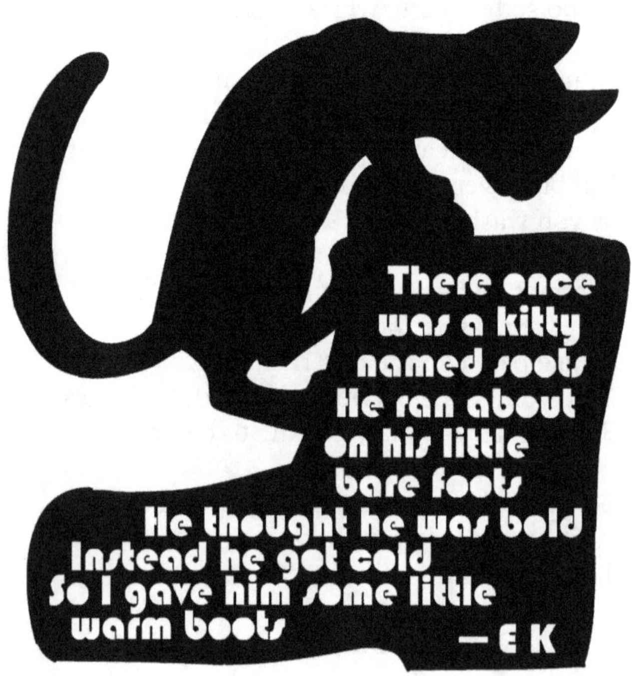

Erin Kennemore

Soots

There once was a kitty named Soots
He ran about on his little bare foots
He thought he was bold
Instead he got cold
So I gave him some little warm boots

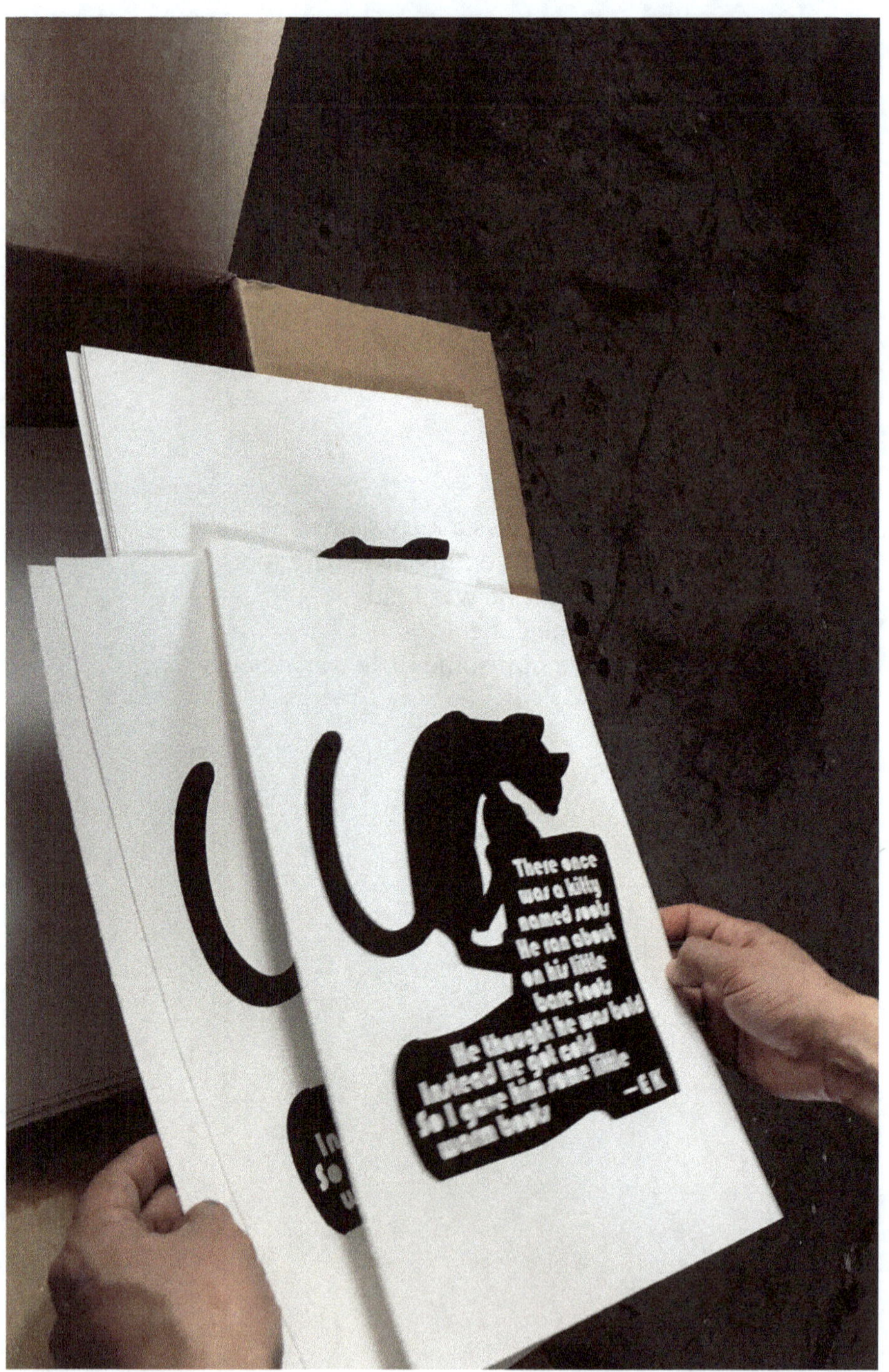

There once
was a kitty
named rooks
He ran about
on his little
bare feet
He thought he was bold
Instead he got cold
So I gave him some little
warm boots
— E K

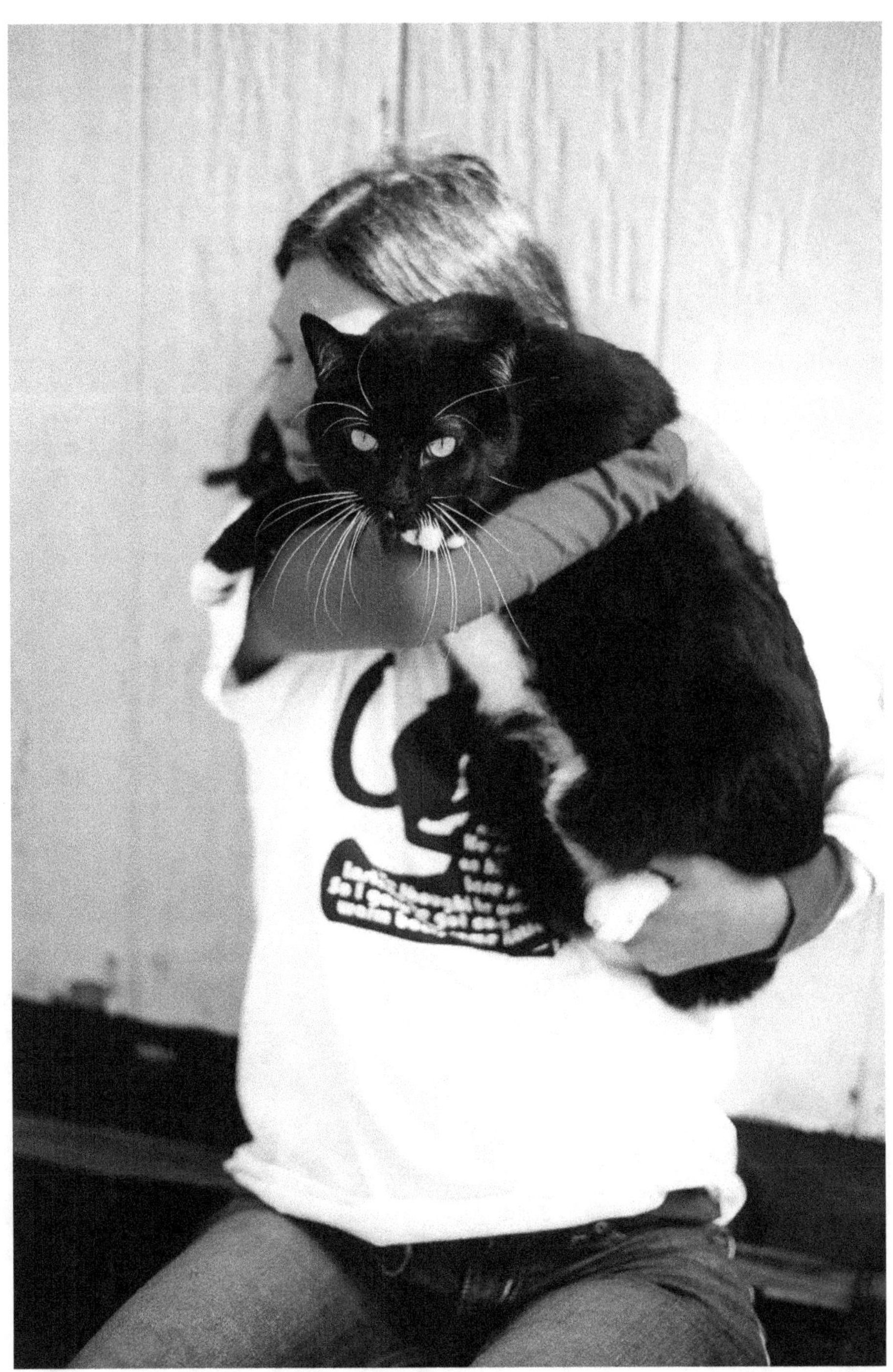

4Lσμ3...

Alexander Shelton

Dementia's A Capella (an Excerpt)

Blue bells weeping, radio-silence creeping,
Onlookers peeking, onlookers seeking.

Here are the flowers of never ending powers, climbing its way through
a heat bended maze.

It's own attack smacks wanted cracks, searching the place for an
unexisting escape.

There's the kindled whipping tearing through married notions. It's
carpeted ceiling rains Contagious peelings of pumped rags.

Balled mites carry inter-vented maps through south. Claiming
heightened flights of discharged Glory, of which sheds clobbered sets of
toned ice.

Darkened paths shiver in boggled pools. Young chants lit gords of
rustic vile, filtering
Oppressed avenus.

Cleaned up.
Cleaned up brushes scratched
Of it's twirled comb, hoping for watt was silent
Joy.

Welp.
Dished battens pounding shorted nots in fead and plead.
They're not what they

Are, for mudded cries howl in decapitated voices.

Benit,

Bent,

Broad,

Bushes, of tangled

Glass-*wire*, clicking
Sharpened clouds

Of,

Nail.

4Lσμ3...

So I await your return
I await your return anxiously
Not the inside
on the chair
My chair
I love you I never stop
You love the people across the street
When you finally return you are asleep
My chair I wait on the chair
Not the inside Why must you leave
Inside You can't go inside
You can't go inside
on the chair
My chair
Inside
Inside
Inside
My chair

on the chair
Why must you leave
My chair
Inside
Inside
Inside

Madeline Lopez

An Ode to My Cat

I'll await your return anxiously

You have to go away so frequently

But why
Why must you leave
Me
I love you
I'll never stop

But you like the people across the street
When you return you are asleep,
on the chair
When you are the one who wants to meet
Inside
You can't go inside
So I'll await you return anxiously
I'll wait on the chair

That looks to the house you prefer,
Not the inside
You can't go inside.

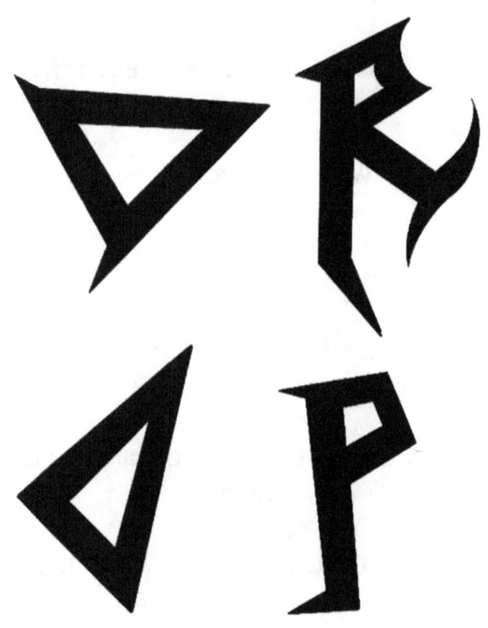

Mia Lytle

The icicle

I watch the icicle let loose droplets down to the soggy wood.
    drop
I don't want to do this, not here, not now
drip
But I have no choice,
            drip
I have to.
                drop
I have so much that I still want to do,
    drop
So much more that I still want to see,
          drop
Maybe I could ride a roller coaster before I do this....
drop
Or just eat good food one last time,
                drop
I know a really good restaurant not too far from here.
    drop
....
          drip
Ugh I do this every time.
   drop
Right when I'm about to drop like the water
         drip
I wish I didn't procrastinate so much
            drop
Oh well, I'm already here I guess
    drop
I secure the rope to a thick branch above
                drop
Using a knot my grandparents taught me
            drop
Before they grew old and it was burned from their memory
              drop
It's kind of ironic
  drip
the knot that once saved me
             drip
Will now be the knot to end me.
        drop
I begin to tie the dangling end
          drop
Into a loop
   drop

And place it around my neck.
                              drop
I look down from the branch I was standing on,
                 drip
Am I really ready for this?
        drop
As I contemplated the sound of splashing grows louder
           drop
It is the only thing I can hear

     drip
And It will be the last sound to echo through my ears

             drop
I position my foot over the void that separates me from the ground,

     drop
The drops abruptly halt.
Like a message from mother nature, telling me to stop.
But what was to come had already been set in motion.
I was already lost months ago.
I tilt the edges of my mouth into a smile
And step off the ledge.

                        drop.

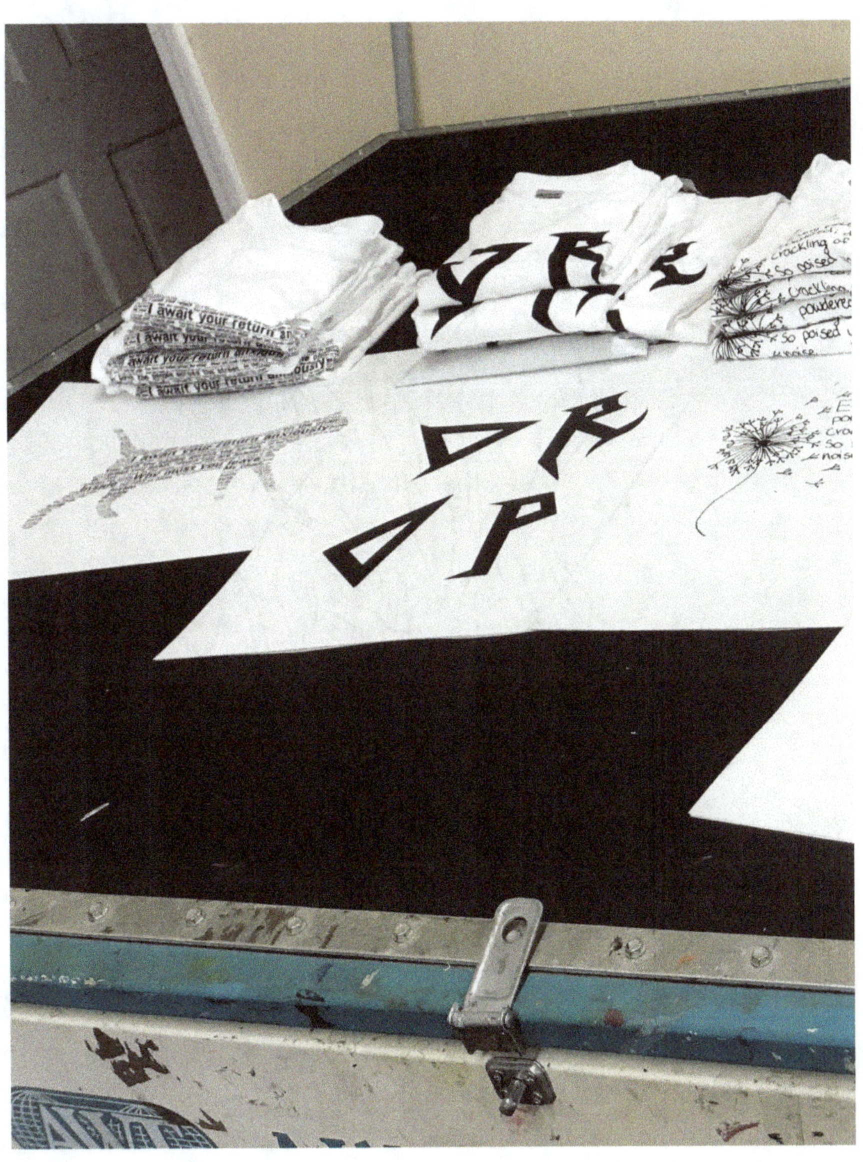

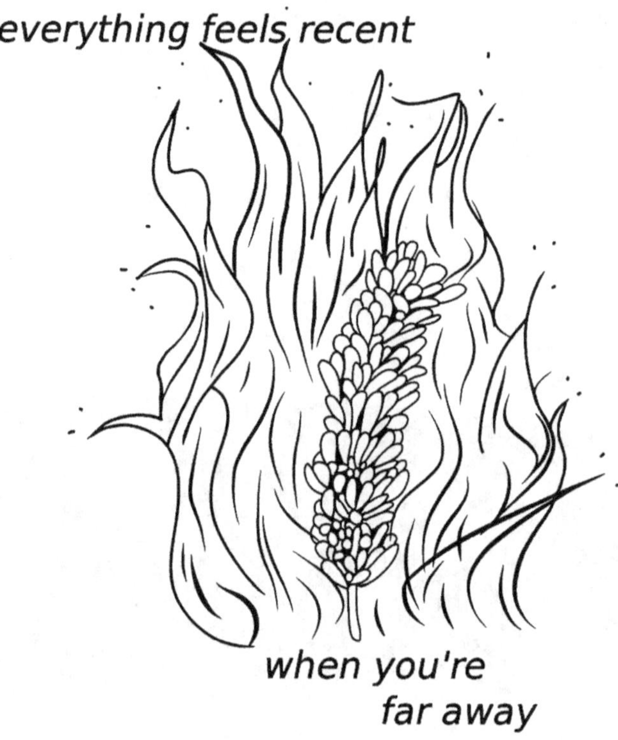

Lesly Esparza

Incense

Blood rushes through my veins
my ribcage burns away
lavender smoke
lifts up into the white
everything feels recent when you're far away
Does an old thing know when a new thing will come?

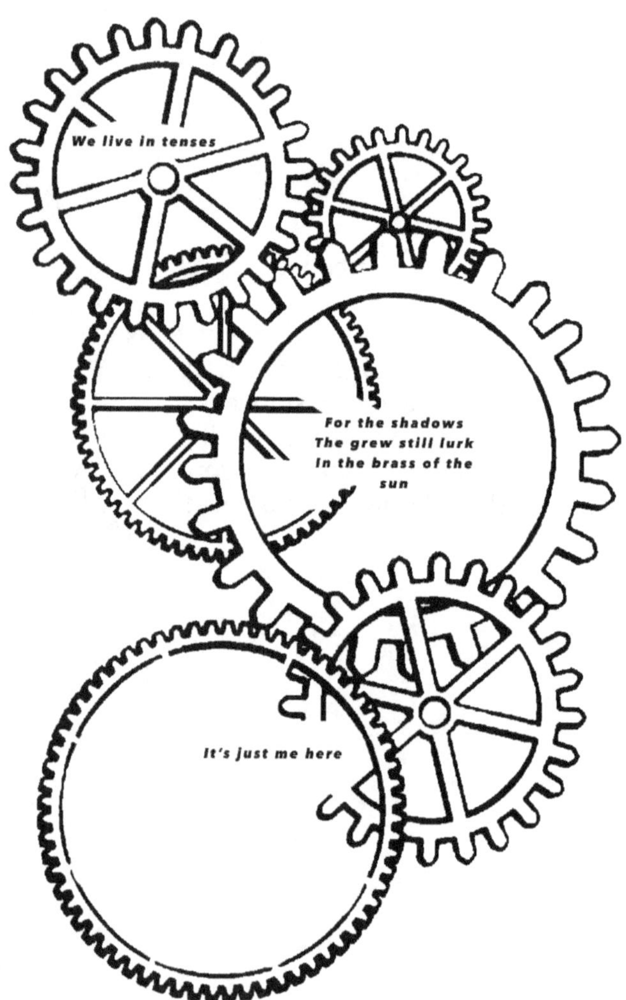

We live in tenses
For the shadows
The grew still lurk
In the brass of the
sun
It's just me here

Neve Naktin

Tenses

We live
In the tenses
You in the past
Her in the future
And I
In the present.

The earth
Rotates, tilting
time crashing by
Like ocean waves
That take
The shore

It is us here
now.

It was us there then
And soon, tomorrow
It will be us
Once more
Because the future no longer
Exists.

The past trails
behind in dust
A shadow
Curving over cement
It's the price we pay
To live one more day

And leave the future
Forgotten.

We look forward, into
The ambiguous anxiety that
Hazes the future phrase
And bow backward to the
Unruly and contagious

Disease of past faces
But we should
Just breathe
The air of the present
Gripping the grass as if
It will die soon. It will.
That's its future-

Though the time it was mowed
Was more painful
For the shadows that grew
Still lurk in the brass
Of the sun.
So I, in the now,
Will breathe the air as if
It will disappear
And will curl my fingers
Into the earth
As it tilts
Once more.

Unclear, because it's just me
here.

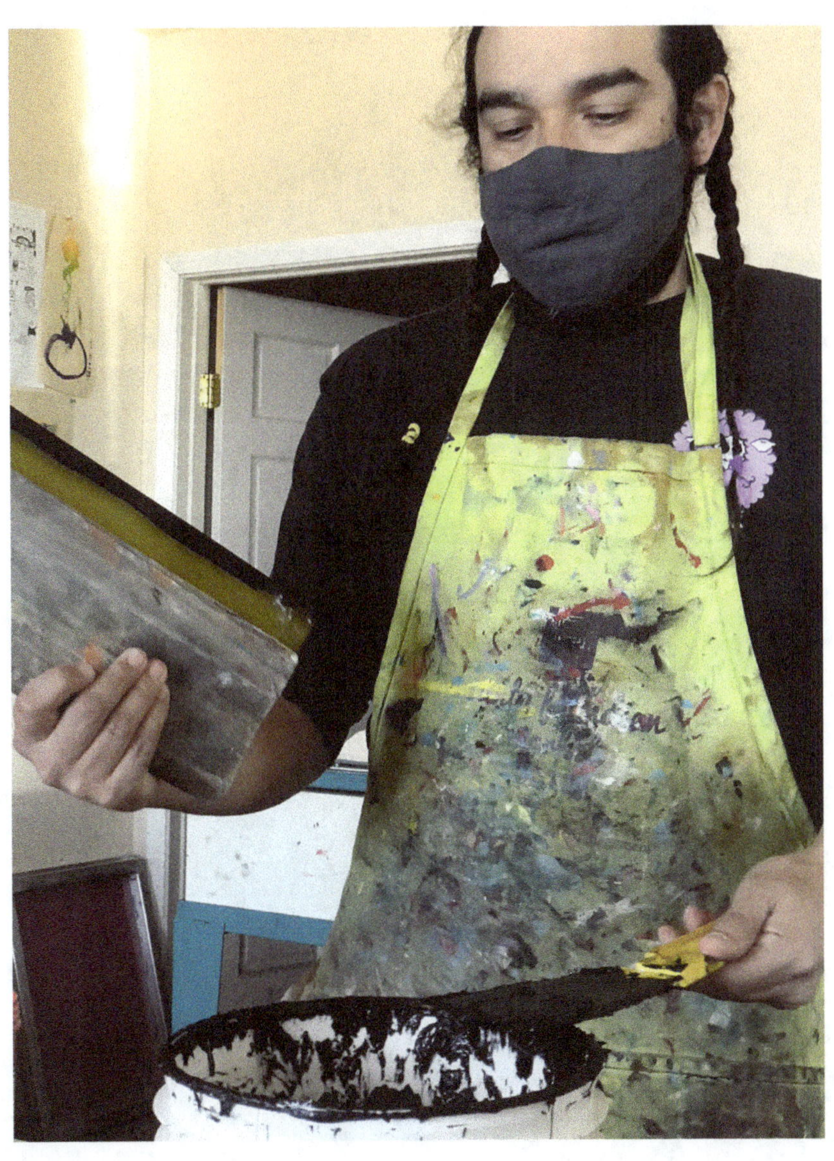

THE CYCLE BEGINS AGAIN

Raven Callaway-Kidd

Springtime Cycle

Sprouts pushing
paving peeling back
thick cuts of earth;
protection from
predatory pantheons
Of pretensed promises,
Oh to give that up
for a self-indulgent show
of abundance in colors, textures, fashions
Forced outward
in a symphony of beauty

Petals bursting
Pollen beaming,
An explosion that tastes,
smells, hears the same as you

For a thing so alive
Deserves the privileges of living:
the voluptuary feast of perception,
and sensuous luxury--
Yet this privilege causes pain
As seeds
Split, tear away from dewy stem
Like crisp pages from a burning book;

Flitting through wind,
Finding their way,
Freeing spring's gifts
To the enraptured world.

Seeds flirt with seeds,
Eggs of flowers,
Eggs of women who bleed
Into the earth-
Browns enrich,
Eggs fill,
Throb with life

As seed dances with egg

In sensual salsa
Barely brushing
Although each craves taste
of other's lip;
This tango of torture
Lasts far too long

Until burrowing
Beckoning, basking, baking
Life ignites! Grows,
Feeding on power,
Resting on strength,
Lays its head on a pit
reserved for guilt

Till head grows too big,
Body gets heavy; and bursting,
Bursting with anticipation,
With desperation
With excitement
With hunger and

Baby!
Born to raw world
Shouting!
screaming!
Unleashing defiance,
Engorging the cycle.

Introducing a fulfilled hell
As only known by mother or father-
As made messes must be mended
And hurt hands must be healed
Faults are fixed and

Minds are mixed by babes
who demand care and love,
playtime and picnics
where mother spreads blanket
and father spreads jelly
And as mother whispers
into father's ear
The cycle begins again

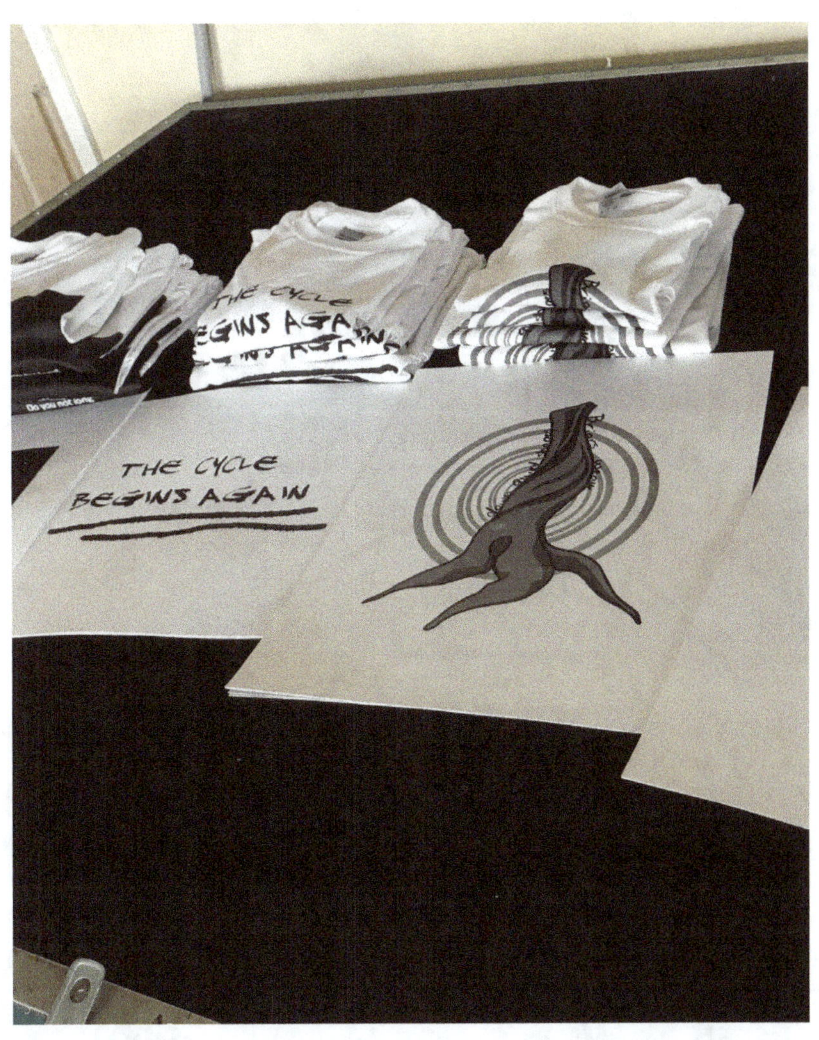

THE CYCLE
BEGINS AGAIN

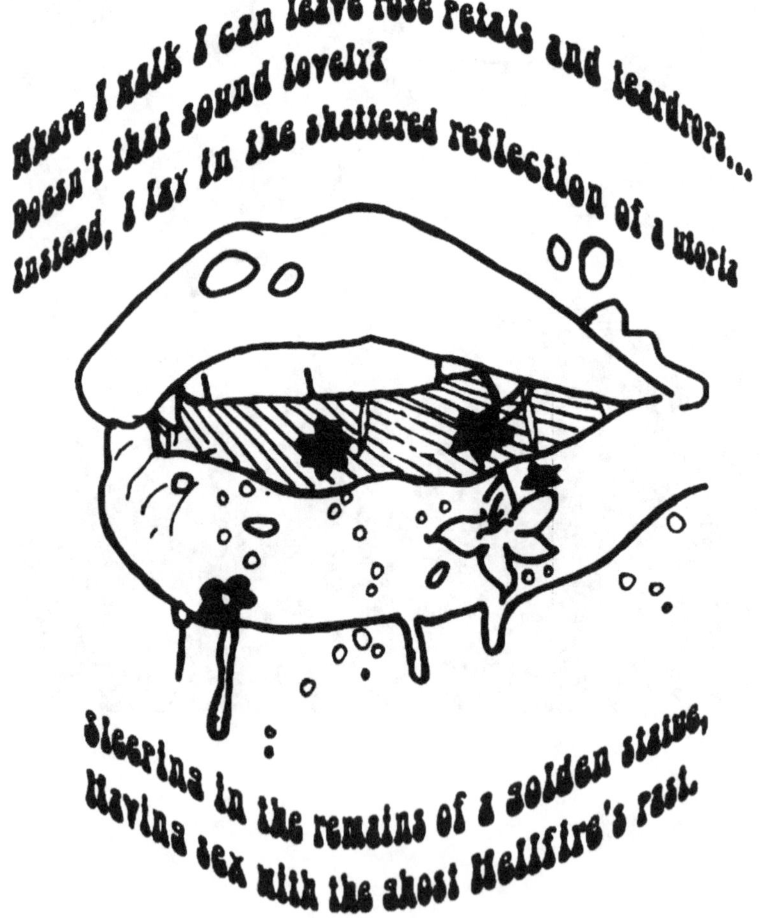

Serenity Medina

I met a golden statue last autumn.
It towered above me,
We were surrounded by these spinning balls of color and blinding light.
They blew up in the background, yet my eyes stayed fixed on you,
Who was hiding in the reflflection of the golden statue's glimmering
eyes?
I watched as the statue began to melt and even as I ran up to it,
My hands and body holding onto what burning gold was left, trying to
keep it together.
You stood there, watching. I could see your reflection morph within the
light gleam of the gold, plastered, and stuck to my body.
I watched as you spread your wings and waved goodbye
I, however no longer have wings.
Rather than chasing you into the sun I stretched out my hands and
blocked you from my vision.
Was it something I said hidden written between the lines of the silence
when our eyes met?
Or my red horns peeking out from my out of control hair?
I hide within the ruins of cities I built.
All I have left of you is the gold from the statue you melted with your
presence
It remains plastered to my body, forever a part of me.
The disoriented piano ringing in my ear is begging for me to grow
wings and file my horns.
So I can chase you into the clouds and take a bite out of your
sweetheart.
My darling how does a golden demon's hand sound on your silver
cheeks and wings?
You brilliant embodiment of everything I have ever felt before
I can be your freak
Where I walk I can leave rose petals and teardrops doesn't that sound
lovely?
Instead, I lay in the shattered reflection of a utopia
Sleeping in the remains of a golden statue,
Having sex with the ghost Hellfifire's past.
Tell me, darling, why couldn't I have wings too?
Why couldn't I fly away with you?

They Flow From the Cracks
Under Closed Doors

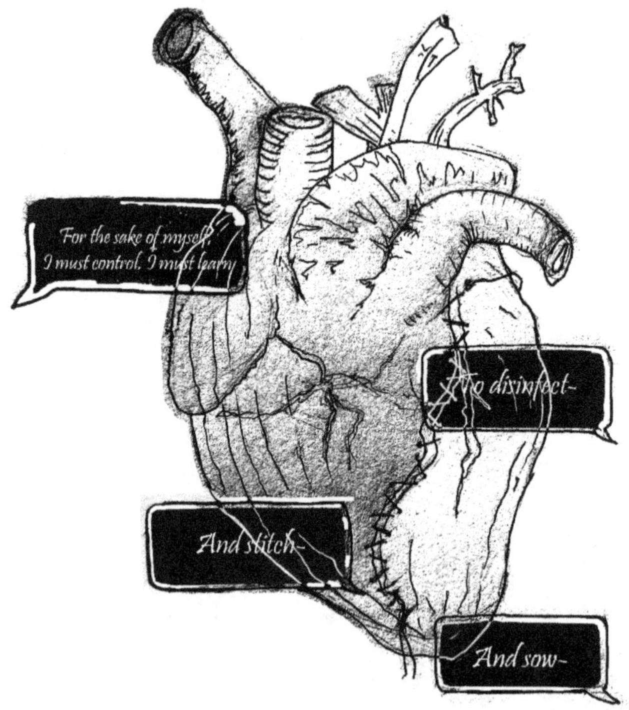

Kathryn Ice-Johnson

They Flow from the Cracks Under Closed Doors

Little testimonies were spoken,
        hints at bereavement:

        •   "He may die" (She said quite casually)

The primal/bodily efforts towards healing dislodged
    and torrents carried them to attack his heart and lungs.

        A one man army.

He returned home
    and suddenly there was clear dependency, which he hated.
He yelled when I stepped on his toes
    and he could no longer rock me on his leg.

        •   "I may have cancer" (she texted to the group chat)

And there was no further mention of it 'till it was done.
Concern became plastered across my face
    and clouded her icy blue eyes.

        •   "It killed his brothers" (she threw towards me)

Since then we have watched him crumble.
His face becomes   thin,   sunken cheeks,   body frail.
My visits became quite unusual, petrified that
                identities/confessions
                                will be left   unsaid.
Every stitch became imminent danger, terminal diagnosis.
Karmic justice towards my behavior.
For the sake of myself I must control.

        I must learn

                        To disinfect -
                            And stitch -
                                And sow -

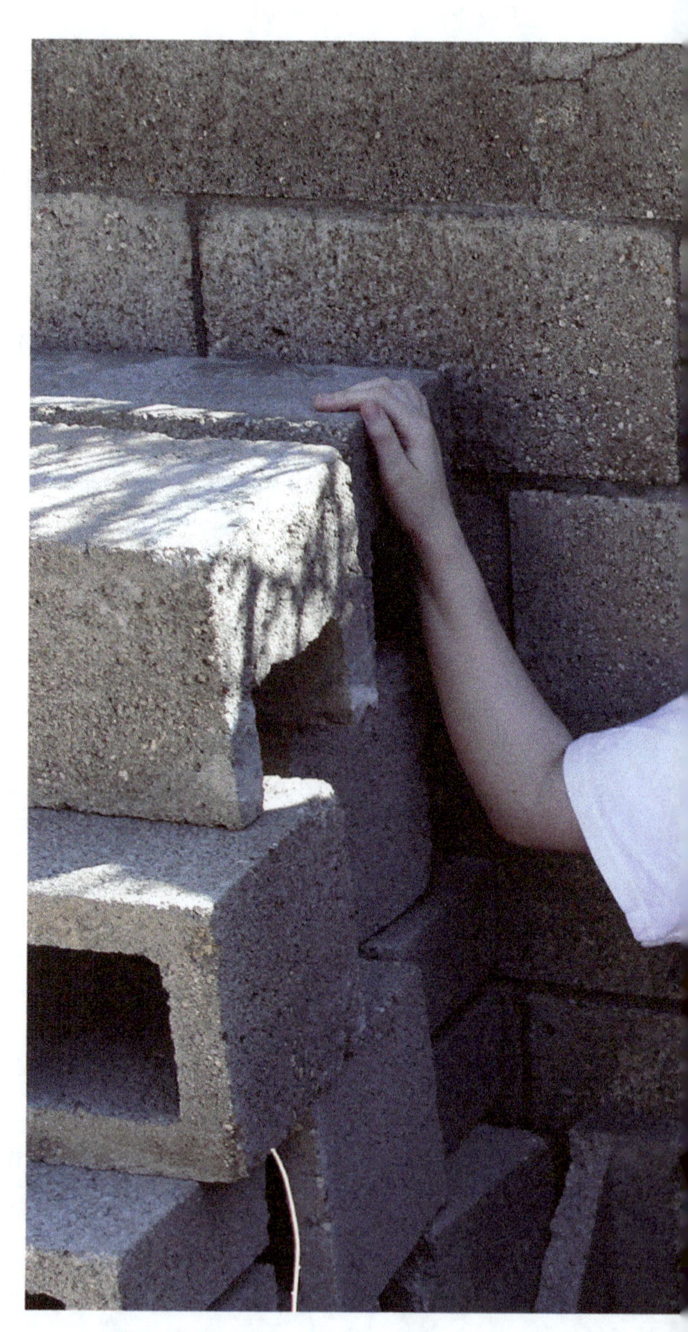

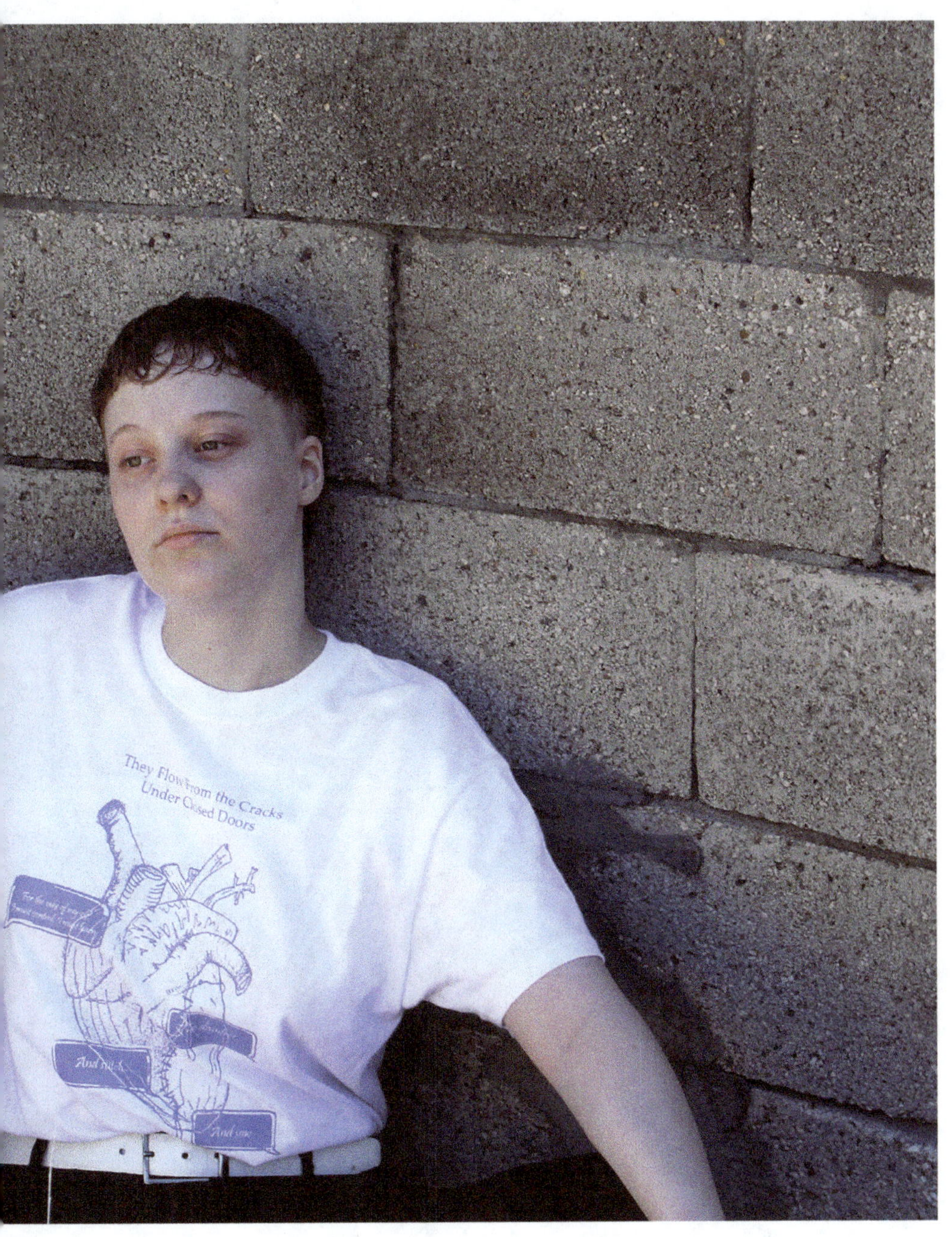

They Flow From the Cracks
Under Closed Doors

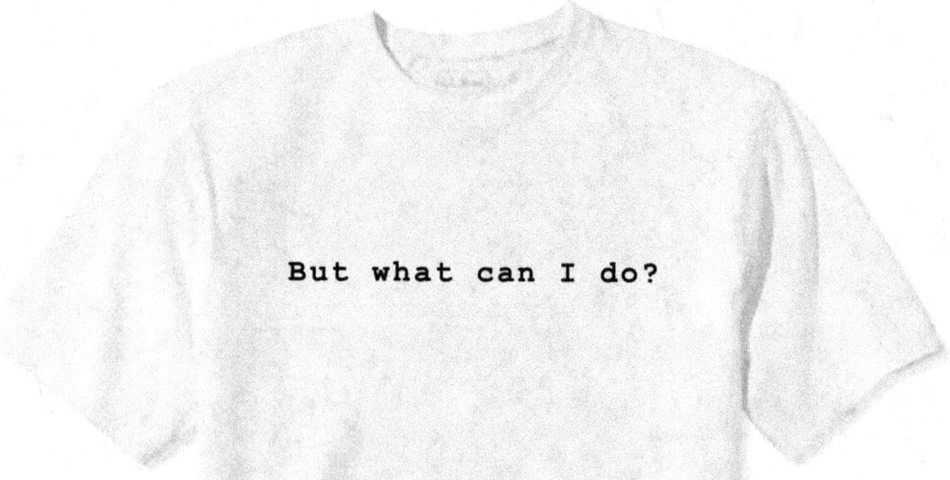

But what can I do?

Alex Odom

One Like

My dad told me about a Russian saying
"But what can I do?"
Their government is oppressive
I say that like it's that much worse than our own, really it's just more obvious
People are pulled over and searched without a warrant
The government is corrupt and the winner is decided before the vote
"But what can I do?"
I guess I just identify with that feeling of helplessness

Normally I would laugh
Seems caring's not past me yet
Even though I say that, what can I do?
Sit alone in bed at 1:56 in the morning?
"One like = one tree saved!"
Fuck, I hate how people will like that post and then have the nerve to say "I'm doing something for the environment!"
Guess it's better than me, sitting on my ass, only complaining.
I can't stand anyone
The deniers, they're not helping anyone
The people who say they care and then never do anything at all to help
Even the ones who are supposed to be "my own generation"
I hate them
How can you put the words of a scared child as a caption to "when ur mom says she'll buy cookies but then doesn't"

Pisses me off, all of it
But what can I do?

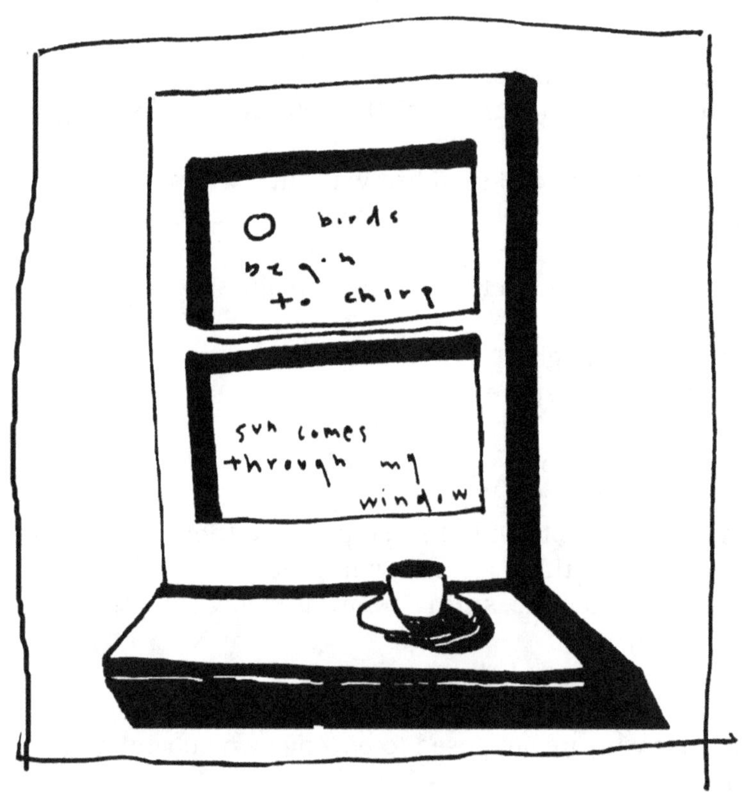

Macaila Armijo

                                        Her arms wide open
                        She finally stays the same
            I can take a breath

Hardly ever burnt
                        The scent almost delicate
                                    Never acknowledged

            A
                    slow breeze passes
                        The rustling of the   leaves
            It gives me chills

        birds begin to chirp
                    the sun comes through the win
                                            dow

                                    just five more minutes

light comes through my fingertips

                                and they're glowing red

                                        rise
                    Relief will   in your chest
        lift   and

                    spread out**ward**   n

                    until u   n   c   o   tai   ed
    lift   n
                    Evaporate into The
                    [Everything/Nothing/Something]

    lift
until feet

Arwen Scarlata

<u>*Open the door*</u>
        and step
            into the night.
                Moonlight illuminates your skin.
                The cycle will end and

                start again.
                Watch The Clouds drift
[in front/behind/away]
                from that lonely piece of the universe.
                You are overwhelmed
                by the desire
                to know The Moon.
So *run* down the illuminated road,   *lift* . . .
lined by sagebrush and secrets,   *lift*   The Stars' gravity
until shoes .   .   . *lift*   will pull you
                                closerandcloser,
                            but never close enough.

                                        Still;

                                    spread your limbs
                                    and catch the wind.

            rise
Relief will   in your chest
and

spread outward   n   .
until u   n   c   o   tai   ed
                                        n

Evaporate into The
[Everything/Nothing/Something]

Welcome to the Rose Garden

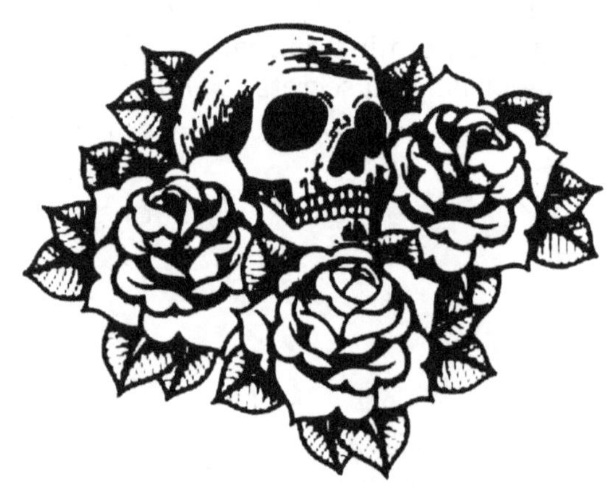

Pearl Cook

Spotlight

blazing fire
that lives in the brain
with white thorns
dripping in blood
Welcome to the
Rose Garden

here we go again
words that never
stop they
come in wet waves
of blue and gray
leaving the yellow
behind

Burn This

Take advantage of **it**

Discard **it**

Whatever **it**

May **bee**

Releasing:

Dreams

Remarks

Expressions

Abstractions

Mellifluous

Songs

Bestrew them —

smoking.

Extricating carbon —

to trees

To breath good life in all

Inhaling the dreams

Of eternal _________.

Gabriel Boston-Friedman

Burn This

Take advantage of **it**
Discard **it**
Whatever **it**
May **bee**

Releasing:
Dreams
Remarks
Expressions
Abstractions
Mellifluous
Songs

Bestrew them--
smoking.
Extricating carbon--
to trees

To breathe good life in all
Inhaling the dreams
Of eternal ______.

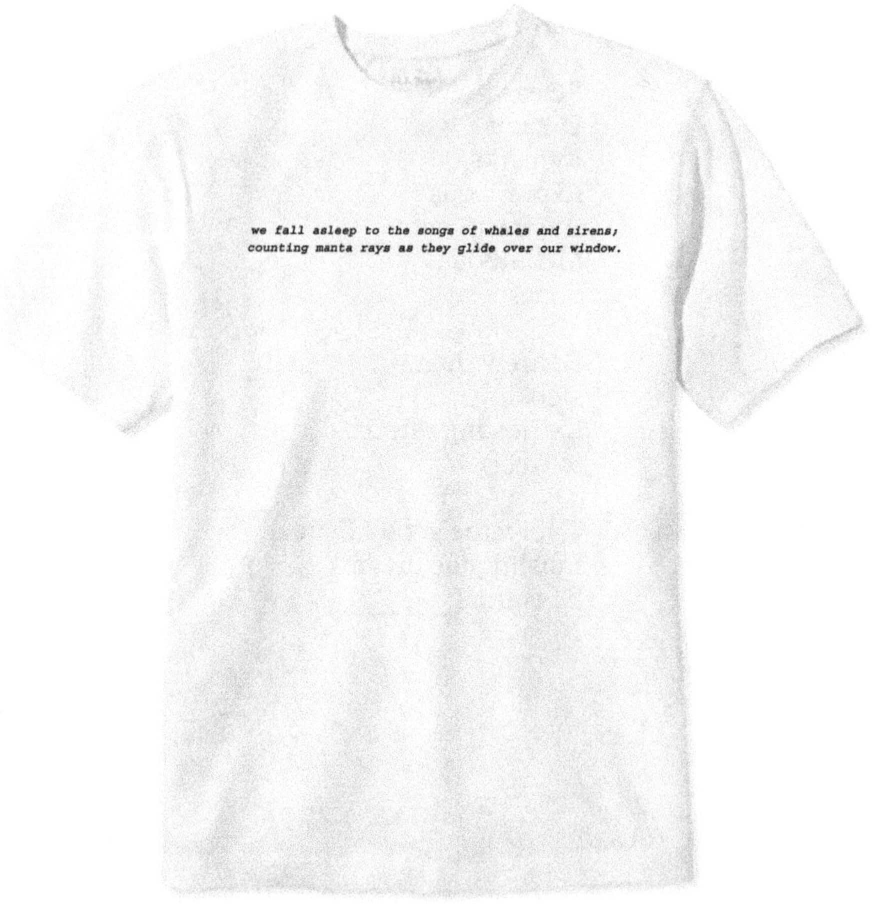

we fall asleep to the songs of whales and sirens;
counting manta rays as they glide over our window.

Sarah Peralta

remember the first time we saw them? cold noses press against colder glass; glass that holds back the sea. we fall asleep to the songs of whales and sirens; counting manta rays as they glide over our window. their backs shine like the stars we cannot see.

we sit in our big glass castle, deep beneath the ocean's surface. cut off from the outside world, we are safe. a kelp forest winds its way around the walls, camouflaging our location.

our stakeout begins with a plastic flashlight from above. your stories circle around my head. I don't know if I should believe you. but why would you lie? I shine the flashlight into the dark depths. the light bounces back at us. we shield our eyes. you take it from me and press it against the glass. a warm ray shines through. the shoal of fish scatter away from it, back into the darkness.

I can't see anything. it looks the same as always. you tell me to wait, be patient. I've never liked being patient. there! you point. I follow your gaze and see her. an outline. her head turns towards us. you wave at her. she waves back. she looks around before swimming closer to us, sweeping the kept away with her steady strokes. you reach your pale hand to the glass, a symbol of peace, a hello. she reaches back, her hand sea green and webbed.

I see you.

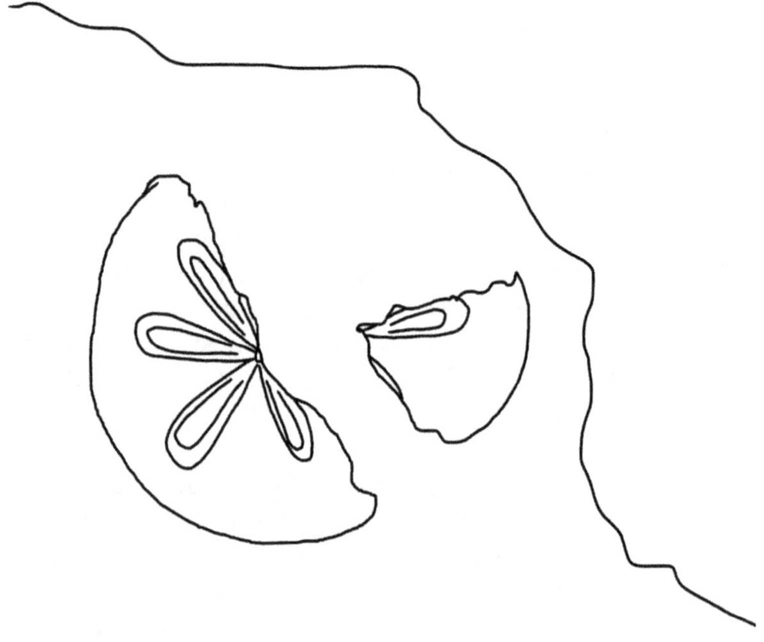

Lucy Wilson

The Brilliant Dark

A storm,
picking up silent petals
of purple lilacs.
He weaves them
into singing cyclones,
dancing them in the valley.
Micro pebbles of sand
leap in rhythm.
Singing a melody of malicious
        Thunderheads.

Green grass seeps into brown
against icy clouds.
Spinning waves of ash
saturate in crisp air,
and crash through perfectly stacked
        Bricks.

Sand eats through the souls
of my shoes—
I run away,
into what was once
        A Sunset.

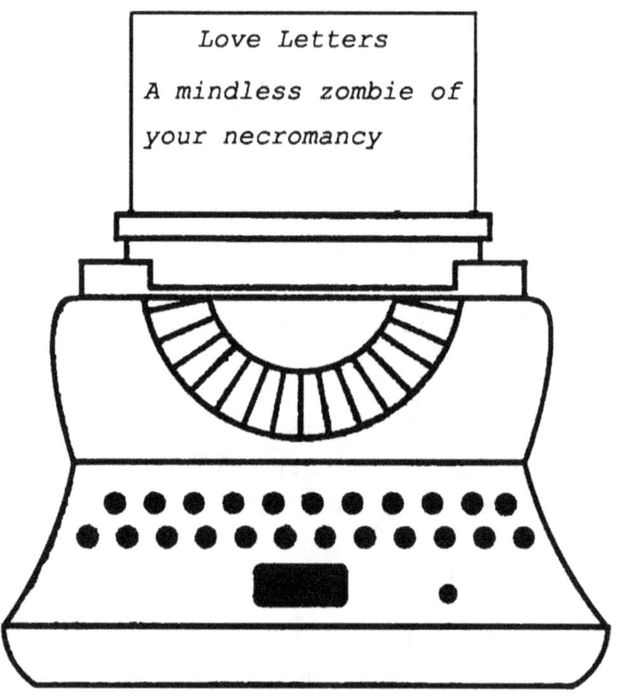

Marco Gallegos-Mikkelson

Love Letter

I'll let you keep a tight grip on me, hold down my body and not let me move. Make me feel weak and powerless. You can make me your servant. Command me. Take advantage of me. You can script what I say, direct what path I should take, I'll be your own little play. Say that I am yours, your property, your object, the trophy on your mantle. I don't give a fuck if you hurt me. Make the pain ride up my body. Make tears flow from my eyes. Even if I beg you to slow down, to give me a break, you don't have to listen to my pleas. If my desires for mercy ever bother you, you can push me harder than before. Show me the consequences for ever thinking that you would give me a chance to breathe. Sink your teeth in me as I wail. If you want you can take a full bite out of me. Take me to the brink of death. Don't let me escape you. Keep me in a cage with the borders being your own mind. I'll be who you want me to be, a mindless zombie from your necromancy. I'll leave everything you give me to scar on my body so that you'll always know that you own me. I'll let you do everything to me as long as you say that you love me.

Love, your property

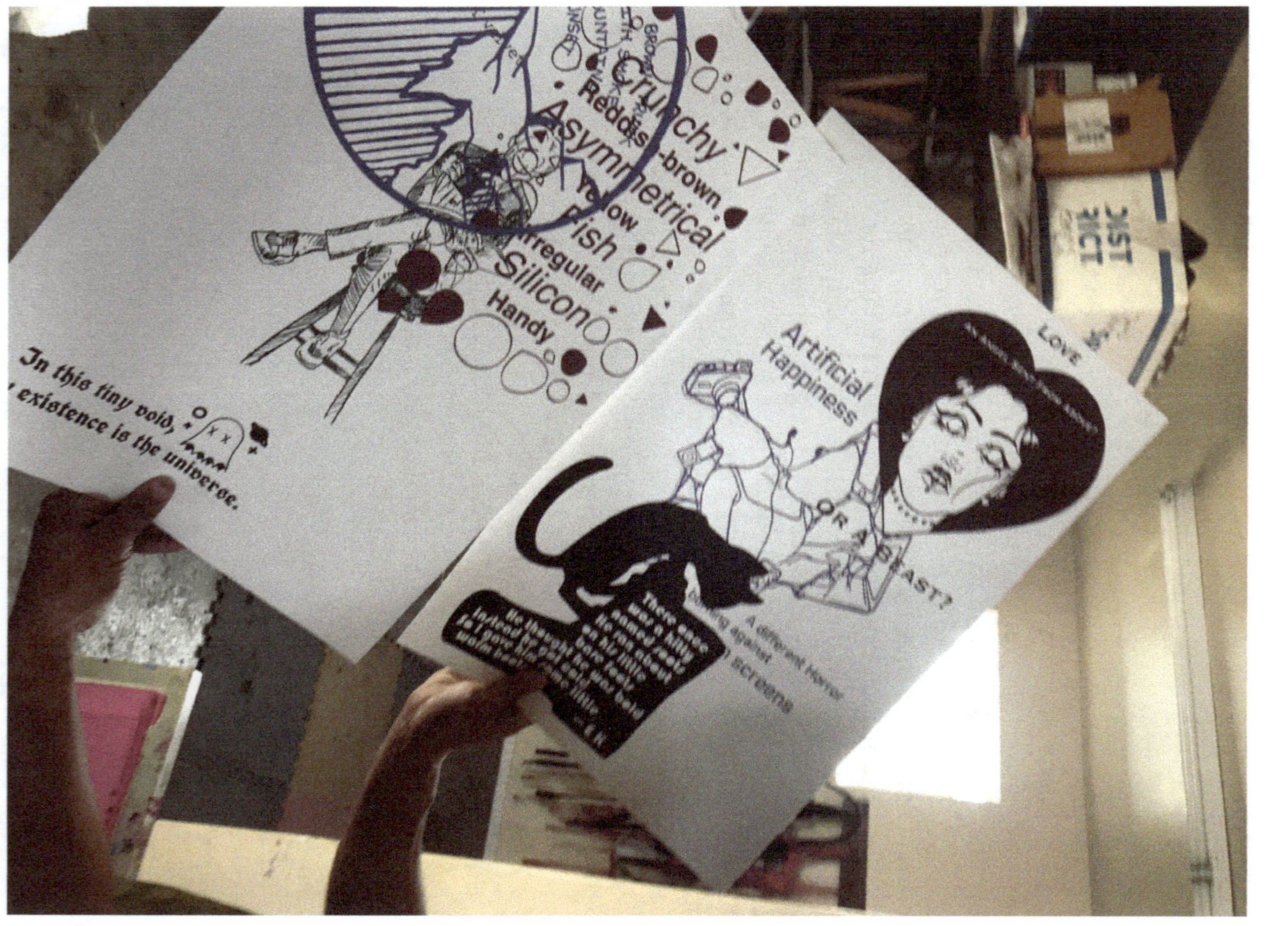
Crunchy
Reddish-brown
Asymmetrical
Yellow
Fish
Irregular
Silicon
Handy
In this tiny void,
existence is the universe.
Artificial Happiness
Love
OR A BEAST?
A different Horror
screens

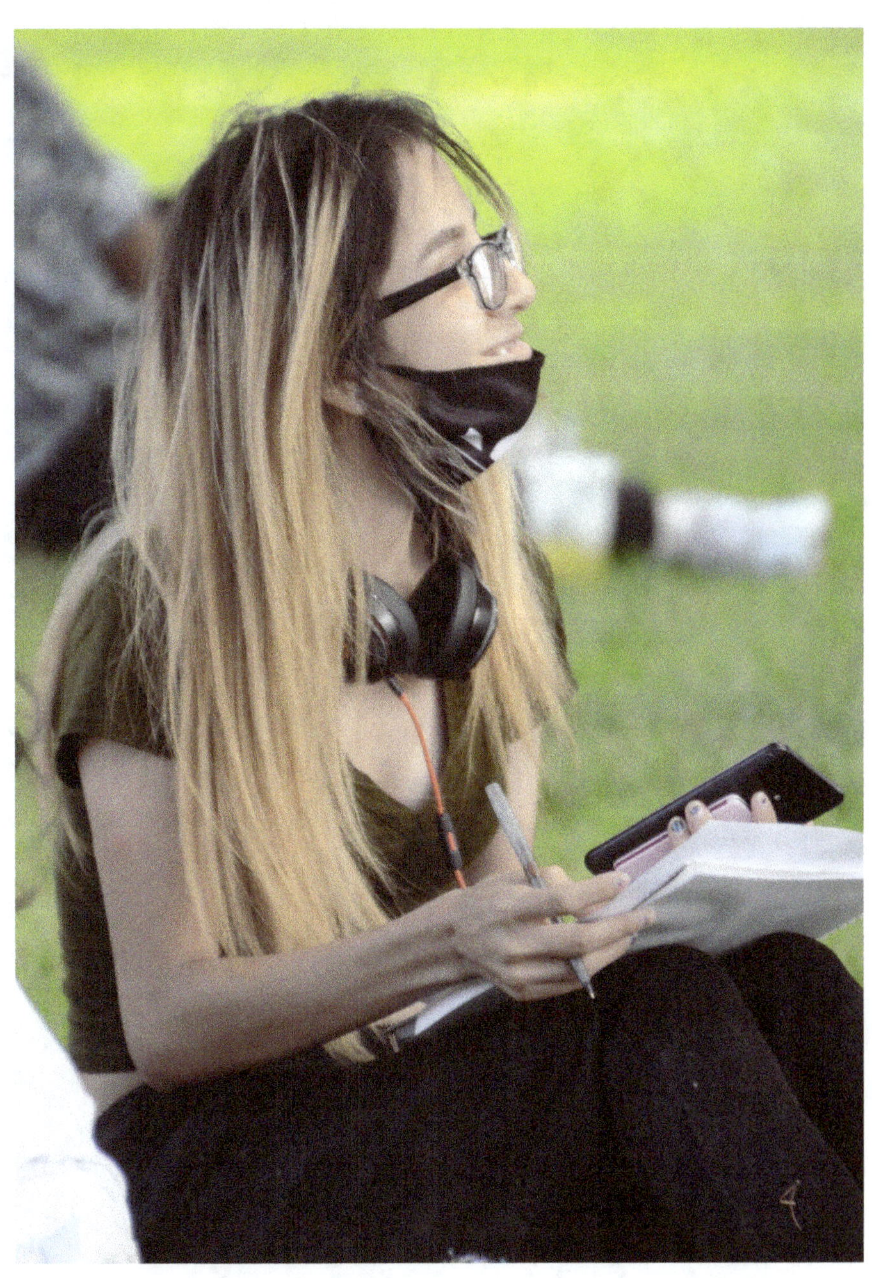

i

wish

for salt

to crawl out

of my eyes if i

can ever feel

YOUR SKIN

again

Oz Leshem

Poem For a Teardrop

     i.   something i needed to say

     the last leech on my cheek i spread my gum into lassitude.
     spit my bone into leisure. rip my flesh from the melody.

to fill a body with goosebumps is to say, a thread woven down the
spine cannot be tethered to another person. but the spigot of your
heart can be spread to each blade of grass growing inside of it.

     ii.   something i needed to write

     a tarnished taboo to be reckoned with. tilted talisman of a
     body. turmoil thawing out your restlessness.

trust in the pen is a tempt shiver. a constant questioning of what
line should go next. teeter, stumble over terse. words become the
task. your throat: tacks and needles. and *one* drop is a good enough
tirade.

     iii.   something that's pulling me
     iv.   scoff scour scorn my insides like cadmium
     bubbling seamlessly throughout my stomach. *steady.* a bridge of
     sham semantics of our synergy. a meander of syntax severing a
     word in half.

confessional dialect emptier than verbiage of what it feels like to
necromance the soil of your body. i wish for salt to crawl out of my
eyes if i can ever feel your skin again.

     v.
a dreamy quiet casted for the two of us. be and i shall hunt for
shelter. the peace is vindictive. a vivid vibration of the kin. my
body. your body a new vernacular the way i monologue over your
tremble. jargon with the garner of your thoughts.

we.   *together.*
and if you shall leave, i'll forever tango with

tear drop.

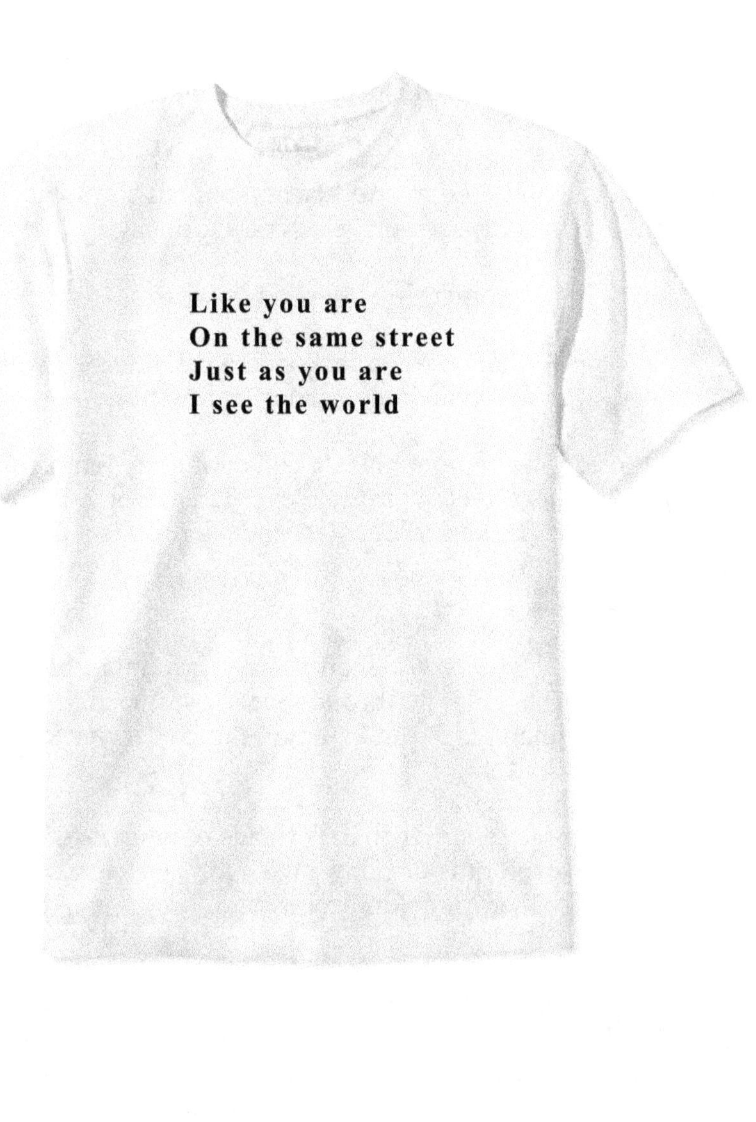

Raven Mackey

Dear Pigeon

Look at all those pigeons!
Fly,
Fly free
Away
Away from me.
Small wings
Street rat
But the people
That make fun of you
They're the street rats.
You
Just try to live your life.
They
Make you live it a certain way
And they
They don't want anyone to make them live a certain way.
So why should they
Make you live
A certain way?
Now I see
Okay
Okay
I'm at the top of the food chain
And yet........
And yet I'm living
Like you are
On the same street
Just as you are
I see the world
Just as you do.
And yet here we are

How
Can
I
Be
Better
Than
You?

Artemisio Romero y Carver

Prayer #50 | *for use on anniversaries and police states*

There was a race in Laguna Park

She tried to tie her laces

before it starts

> She had had those red tennis shoes, they weren't ruby *slippers*
> So she ran on foot when they blew the *whistle*
> and threw a bullet right through the *window*

there was a race | and East La | went to the *victor*
I was an idea | 3 made-up states | and 33 *winters*

> aways, but anyway

still, know the rhythm

> could name the route,
> got the same shoes, tailored suite, my baby loot,
> the instinct to run is a sacred tune,
> a ringtone as loud as they can aim and shoot,
> I get that call, I just pace the room,
> that's a lap on track we named into

don't get to choose your mark,

get set you to know who starts

ahead, the race in Laguna Park

If we stand, no longer
alone but together, we
can make a difference.

Shayla Lovett

Ode to dirt

Dirt has seen it all
 it's felt things nobody understands
It's felt the pain in people's feet.
Dirt is me I feel pain and know dirt's pain
 i know countless people's pain
But dirt is also beautiful
 it grows plants and helps us stand
And when we no longer feel ready to walk alone
When we're afraid of what might come next
Dirt will hold us up
Dirt gives us a lifeline to connect to
And what do we give it in return,
burn it,
Poison it,
Destroy it,
Dirt is a part of us and if you hurt it
You hurt us.
But if we stand
 no longer alone, but together
we can change

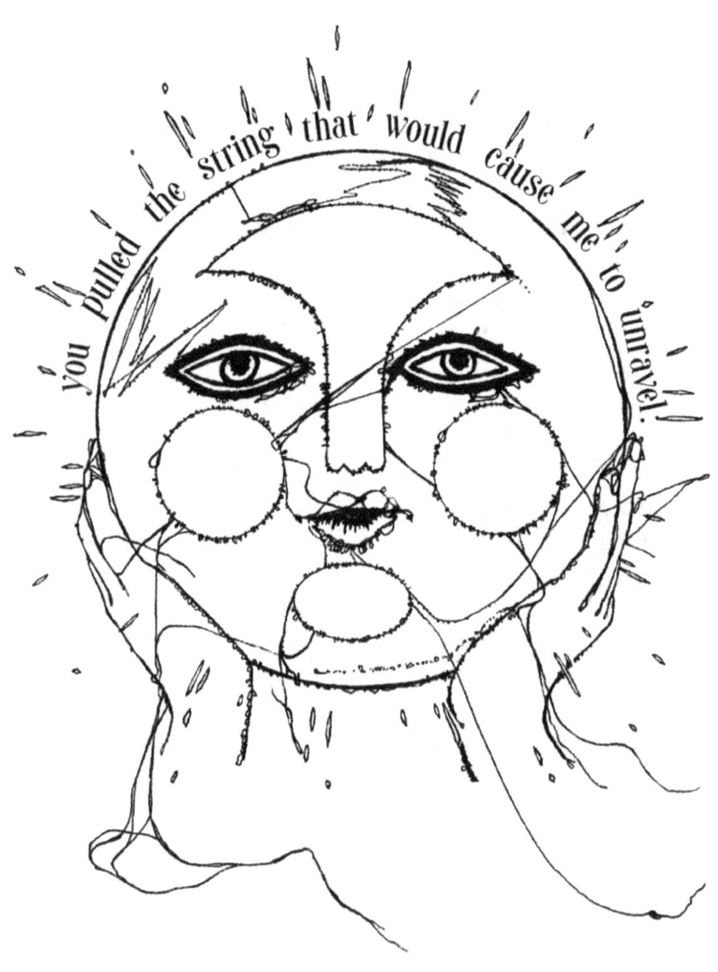

Genesi Sedillo

The Lantern Bearer, Part I

The night served as my curtain,
casting shadows over my dips and curves,
Hiding the seen and unseen behind liquid obsidian, casting a mold
Just as the soot at Pompeii ate the loved and the unloved just the same

And I was satisfied

Satisfied to feel the cold lips of my linens kissing the folds
and divots that I hide with a spring cotton dress
that my grandmother gifted and hid
behind a ribbon for my 16th birthday

The green one, the one that ties so sweet in the back and hugs me
just as you did when our lips first met
We saw the future, but not far enough
under that dying willow tree

Now I can only see the signs,
Omens left behind by the scavengers looking
to pick at the carcass of a long dead dove

The raven stalked us:
watched and taunted.

Just like that owl
when you took me by the river,
the gushing water hushing our declarations of never-dying love.
And I held your breast to my breast,
stealing my breath as it hitched;

you pulled the string that would cause me to
                    un
                      ra
                        vel.

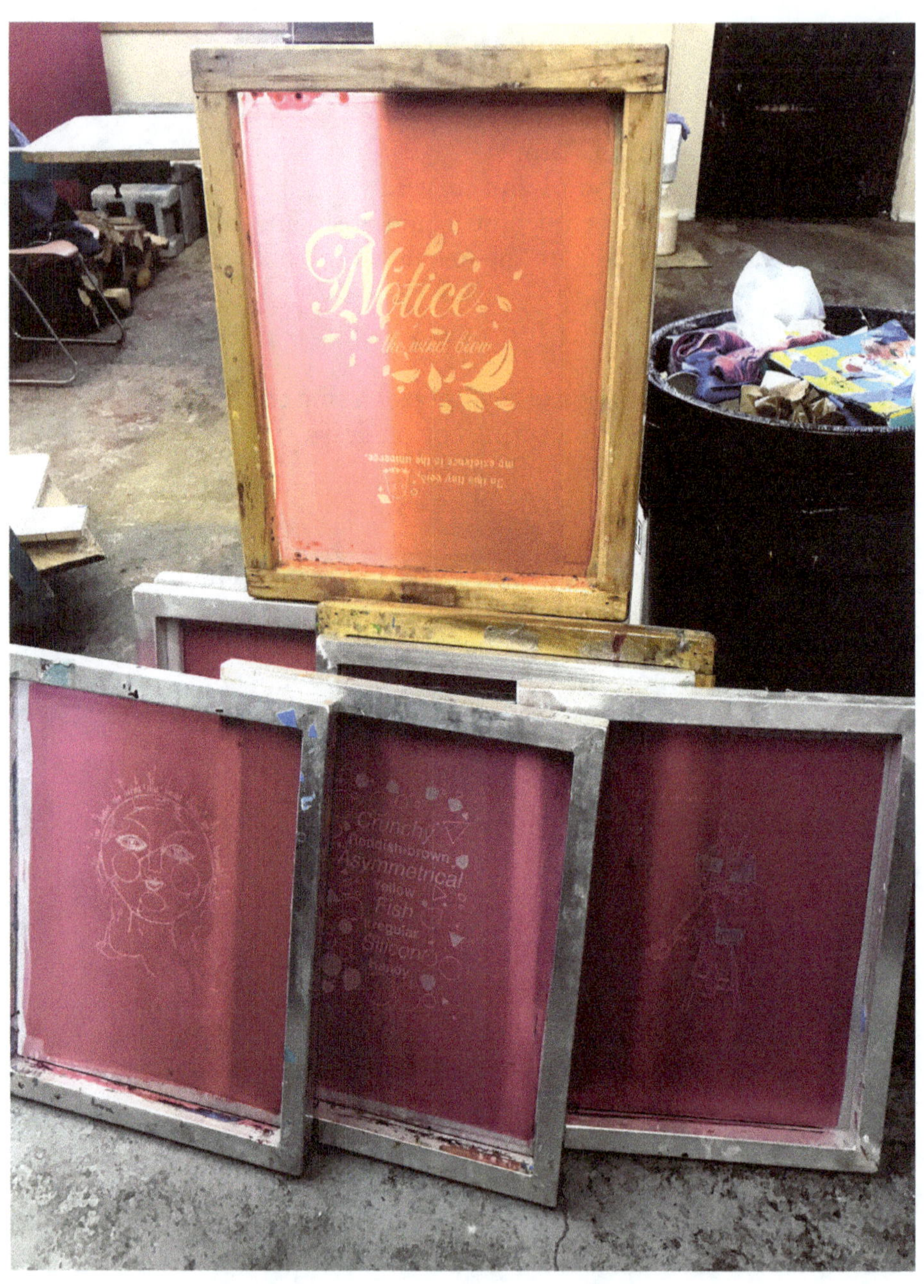
Notice
the wind blow
Crunchy
Reddish-brown
Asymmetrical
Yellow
Fish
Irregular
Stringy
Savory

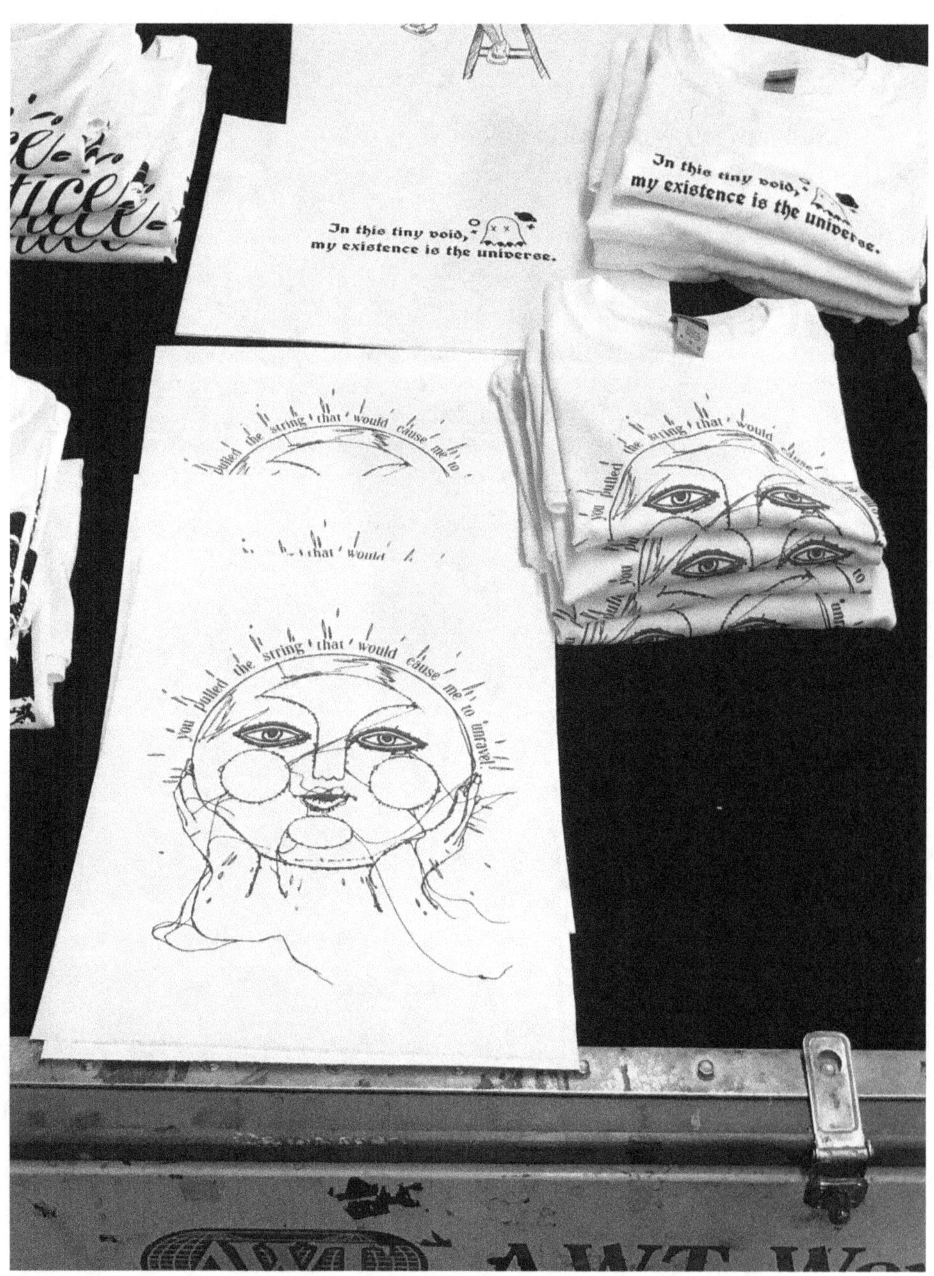
In this tiny void,
my existence is the universe.
In this tiny void,
my existence is the universe.
you pulled the string that would cause me to unravel
you pulled the string that would cause me to unravel

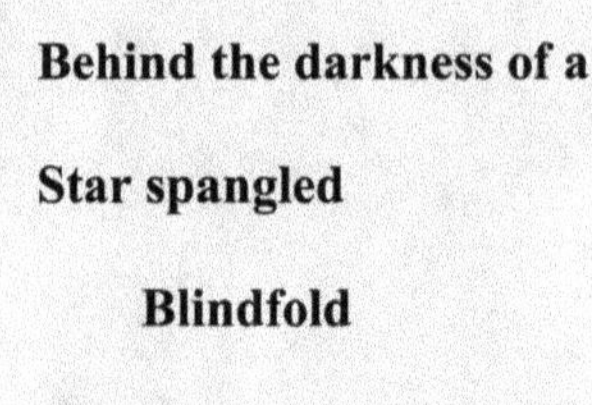

Skye Bowdon

Salvation

       our

  nation under whose

              god?

mine is unproven

regardless,

we want to believe in

              halos

              sanctuary

              bliss

where is your purity

amongst

              smog?

ashes rise

fire

              consumes

effortless savior

              will never

              deliver

while we   cower

behind the   darkness of a

              star spangled

blindfold.

Artificial Happiness

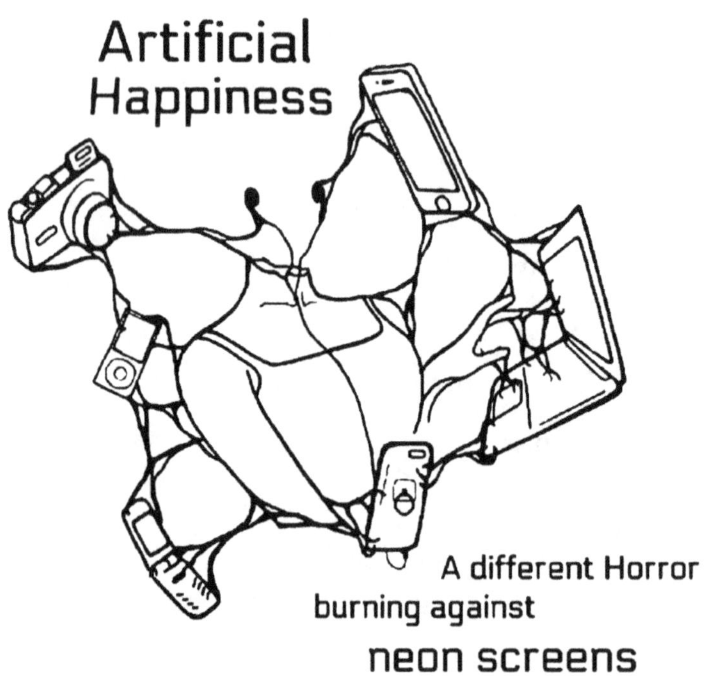

A different Horror
burning against
neon screens

Ella Seckler

Artificial happiness

I went on a journey of knowledge without expectation.

       Awaiting me was
  vast chaos;
  Overwhelmed with thousands of glowing screens

      A different horror burning against their neon lights.

      A silhouette from the warm amber light

      A delicate glass existence burning to break free

     The meaningless memories to those who knew me
     My entity bottled as another pill to be taken and forgotten

     Swallowed in this shattered darkness
                   My head
             is getting heavy,

    with every double tap of my callused finger.

       I grow tired,

    But even in a breaking world;
    A single pill can help heal the pain of a poorly threaded wound.

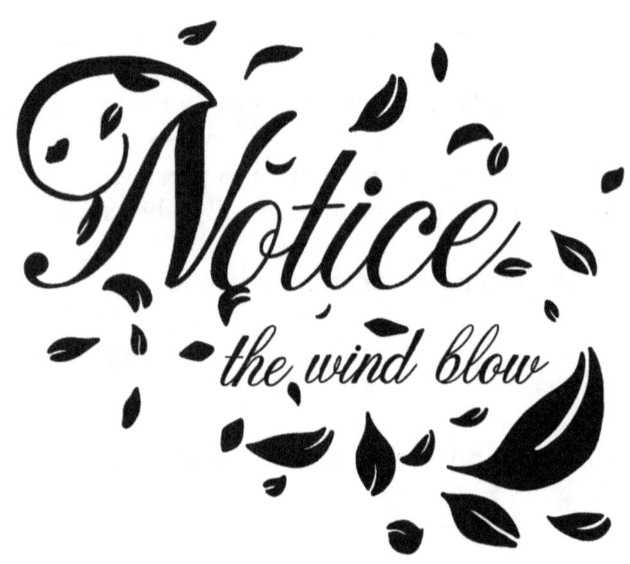

Gina Como Mosconi

Notice

Focus on the feeling
                of when you first wake up
         When the light
                        fills your vision
The comfort and warmth of your bed

Remember the sound
                    of the rain hitting the ground
The smell when the storm is finally over
          The rainbows peeking out of the clouds

Or the warmth of the fire on a freezing day

Notice
          the rustle of the leaves
When the wind blows

Focus
        on the small joys of life
May happy thoughts   guide you
                            For   days
                                         to   come

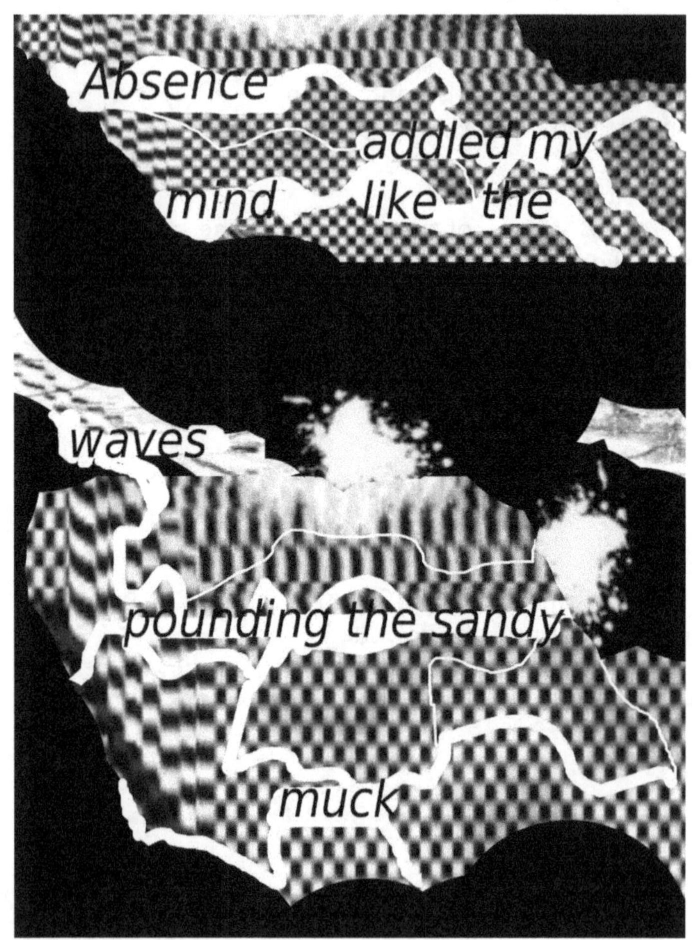

Isabel Somma

Oceans

                                        If you were to die,

                                 what would I do?
Well, the beach is an option,
                        I would imagine what could have happened

  My tears would disintegrate into the layers of sea foam,
                Facing the vast ocean, it reflects back to me,
All the ashes and flowers left to be swept away
And bashed into the cliffs once more again.
  My face wet with tears of dread,
Misted with the cool water droplets swept from the waves
  Hitting the rock cliffs.

  Absence addled my mind like the waves pounding the sandy muck.

    My thoughts blank, sparse but ferocious as the forceful waves,
  Do I forget what we had,
      Or do I remember you wiping away the mist from my face

    Listening to the crashing waves slapping
Water across the sharp rocks
    I remember the late night deep conversations
                However, how would I know if you remember?

                    You're gone, but not in my memories,
    I can't ask you, but I can remember for the both of us.
So I will lay my memories and my flowers in the water
  What I remember about us will never leave me,
            but I will be bold and pursue my life.

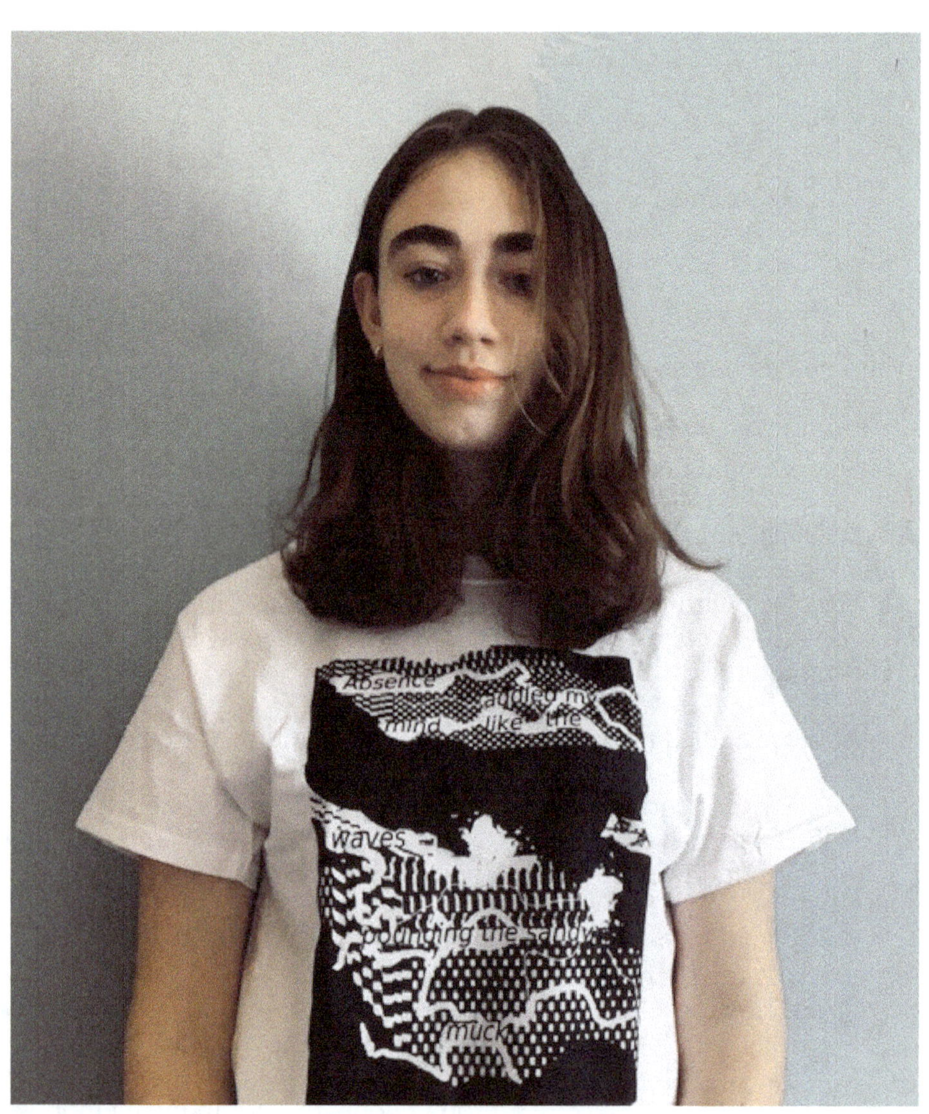
Absence
addled my
mind   like   the
waves –
bouncing the sand
muck

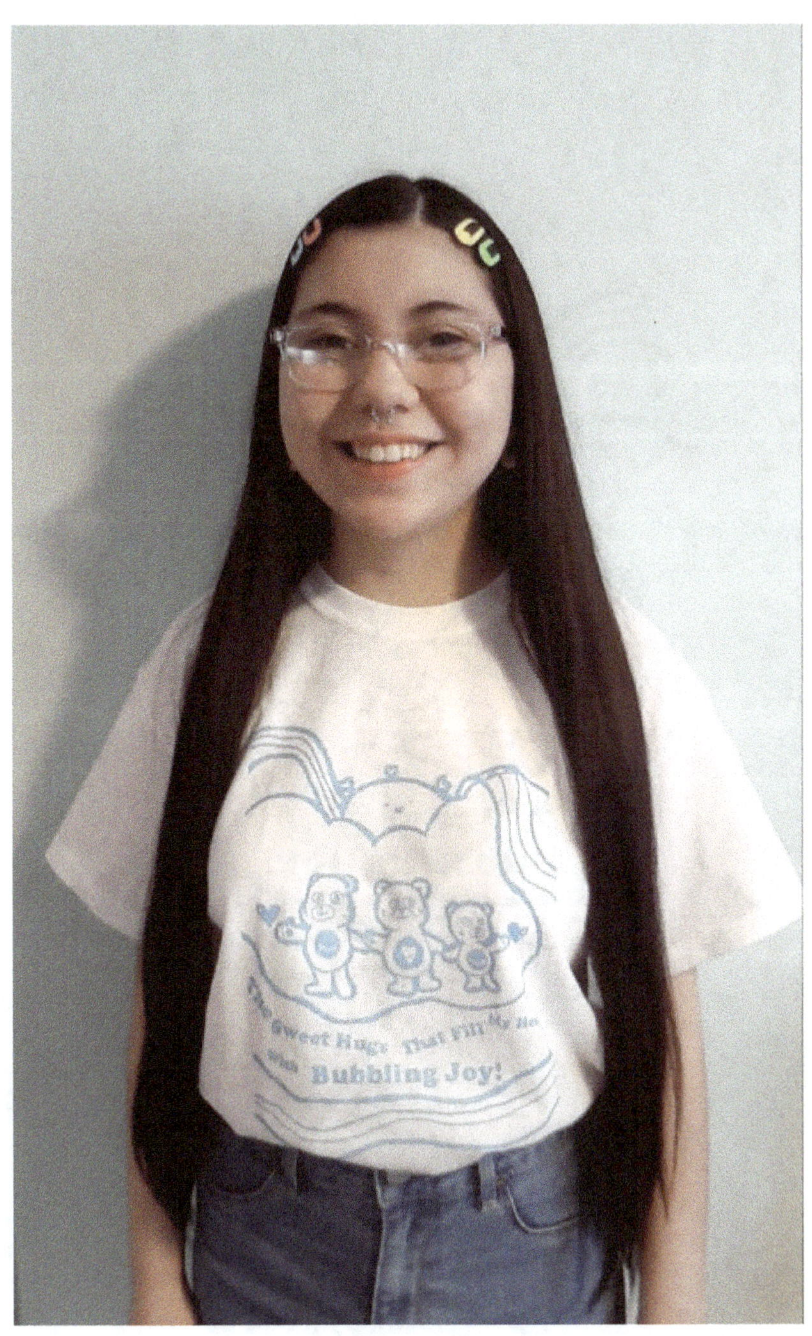
Sweet Hugs That Fill My Heart
with Bubbling Joy!

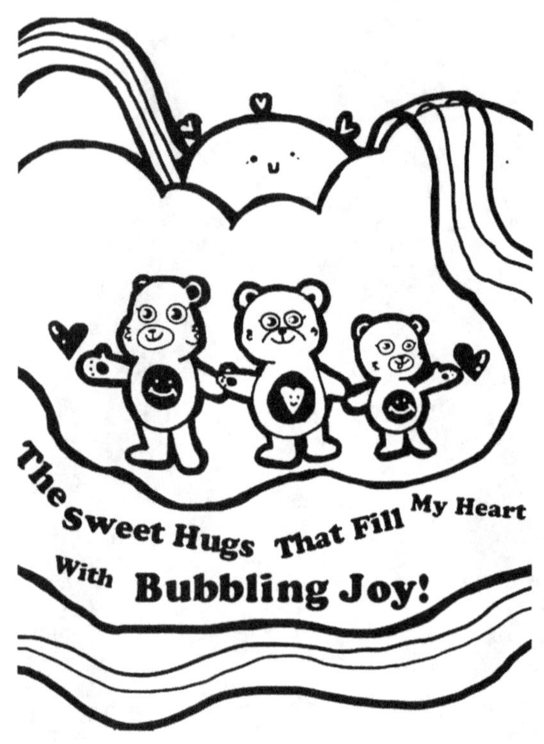

Claudia Marin

Together Like Chicle

Mis hermanas son mi mundo
And yet with all of the time in the world there is no better way of
Spending it than with mis hermanas.
Como la chicle que soy no me puedo separar from the
Sweet hugs que fill my heart with such bubbling joy.

The endless drives full of chatter
The sounds of the highway have always been a great joy to hear
oh how many tears of joy and sadness
We have shed en este zapatito que huele tanto a fresas.

As I write this I recollect all of the sugary memories
that have made my life oh so sweet.
Mis amigas para siempre, my glue, My reliable crew
I adore you and forever will
Las Amo

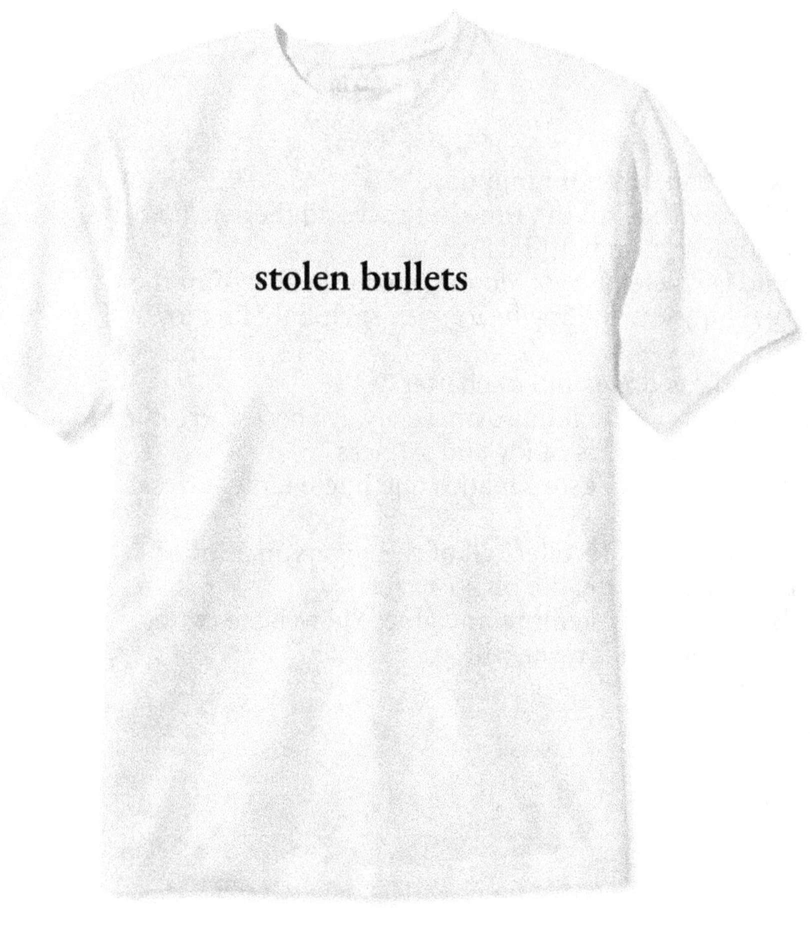

stolen bullets

Nevaeh Galaviz

stolen bullets

i can't focus
i can't breathe
if everything i do

isn't in threes
oh please
don't be looking at me

i wish i could scream
but then they would notice
me counting to three

when there is a bang at the door i drop
like the three stolen bullets that made my family rot
and just like that my mind was not

i cannot think i cannot breathe
i am without an ounce of glee
please tell me how must i proceed

if everything i do turns to dust
how must i proceed
if everything i do isn't enough

the love we spread just turns to must
and everything we do is never just
what must i do what must i say

i've had enough
don't make me stay
i'd rather leave

In this tiny void,
my existence is the universe.

Kory Wagener

Thoughts From The Void

Heart beating with the blood of past lives

            I'm spiraling
                    down a dream
                            I can't wake up from

Remembering who I was or should've been
In this saturated coma of a world

And yet,

                                                    in the end
                                                    I realize

The coma's too l   o   n   g, the world too b
                                                    I
                                                                    g,

For me to dwell on blood stains that don't exist

                It's terrifying to understand that you don't matter,
            And yet somehow the most freeing thing you could ever know

In this tiny void where my
                            existence is the
                            universe,

Anything goes,

And everything will.

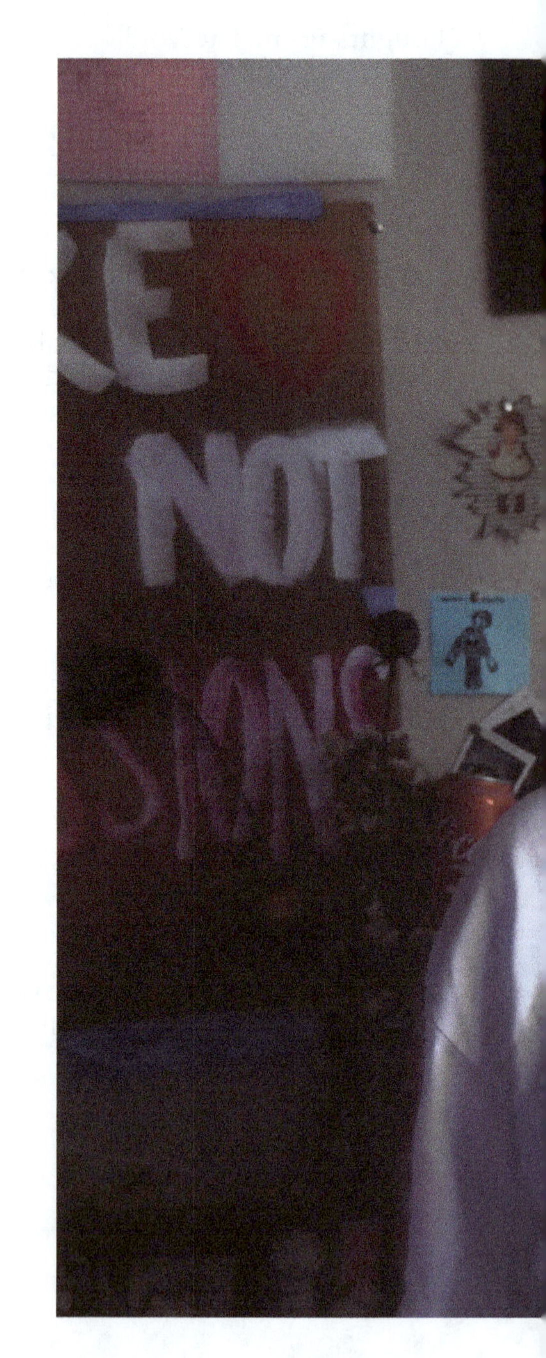
RE
NOT
OING

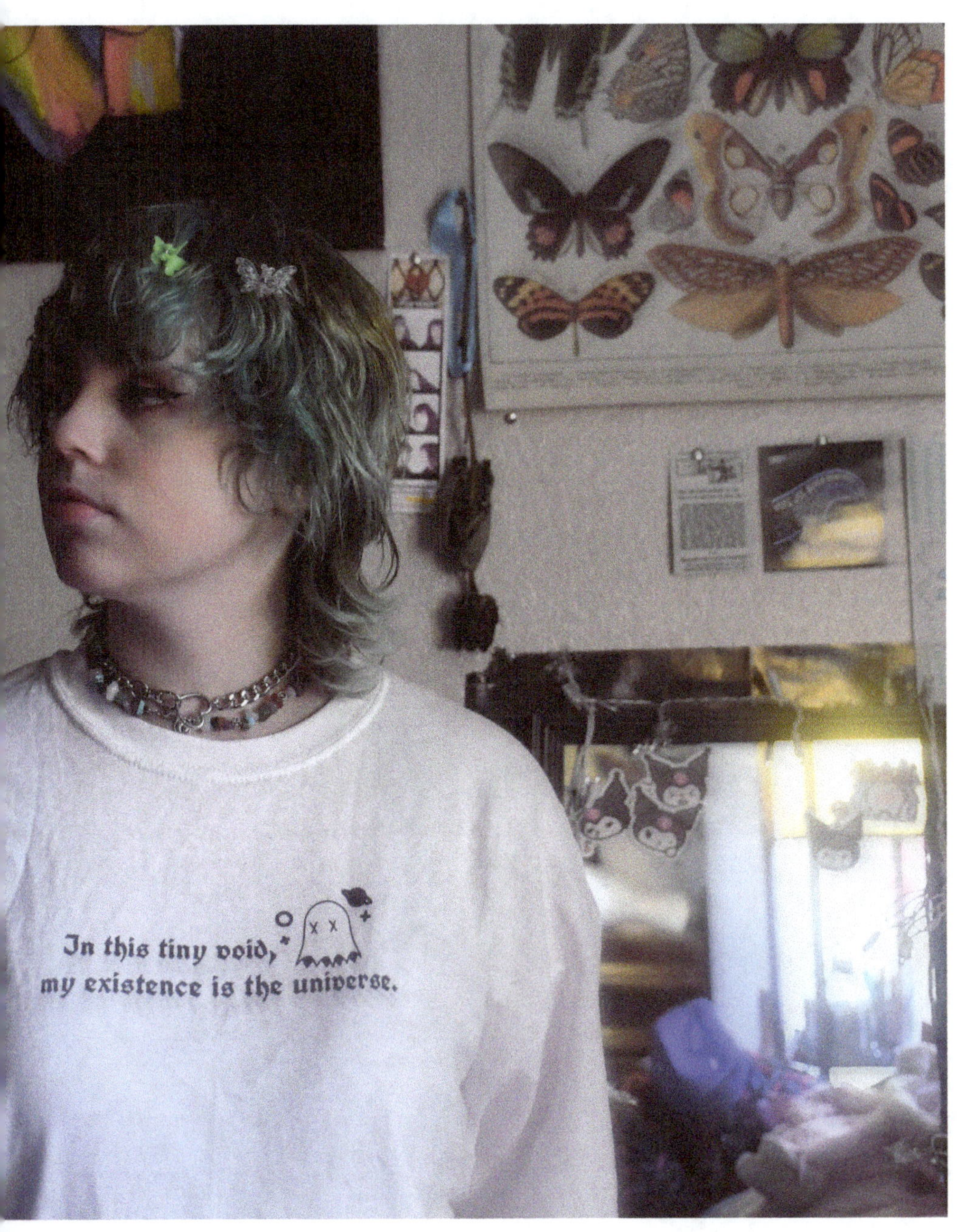
In this tiny void,
my existence is the universe.

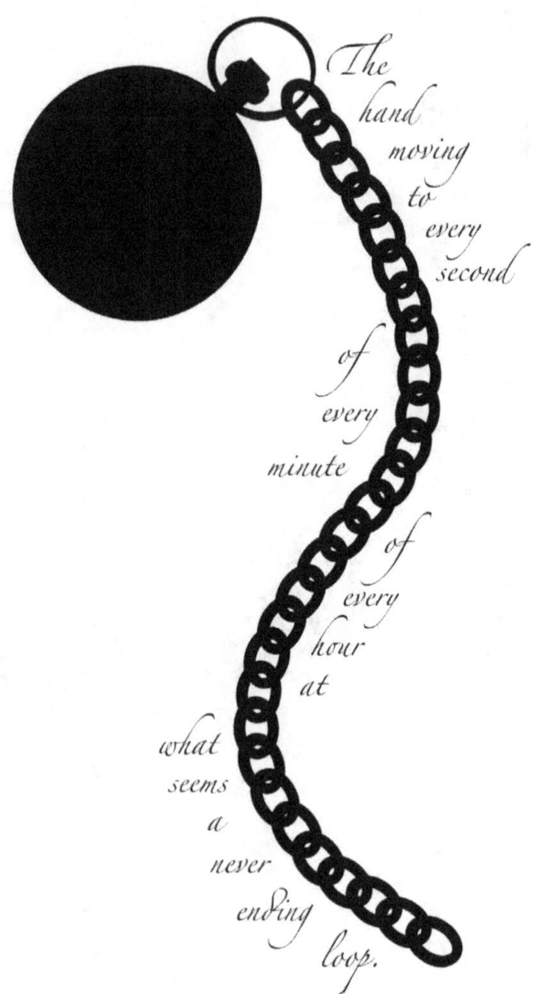

Natalie Baca

The Pocket Watch

The gold surface reflects any light that touches it as time ticks away
The surface patterns making whomever laid eyes on it
wonder what they mean.

The hand moving to every second
of every minute
of every hour at
what seems
a never ending loop.

But every Time Keeper has its breaking point,
from wall clocks, to your average pocket watch.

Someday this
gleaming pocket watch
will have its breaking point.
But till then, it sits in your pocket waiting for the end of time.

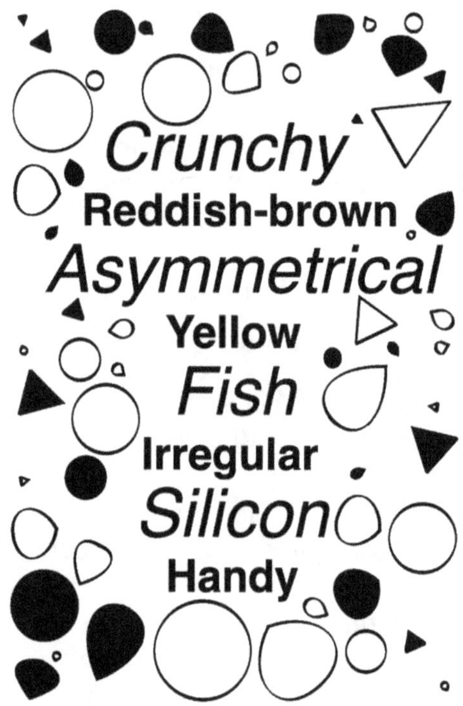

Ray Palomino

Crunchy

Reddish-brown

Asymmetrical

Yellow

Fish

Irregular

Silicon

Handy

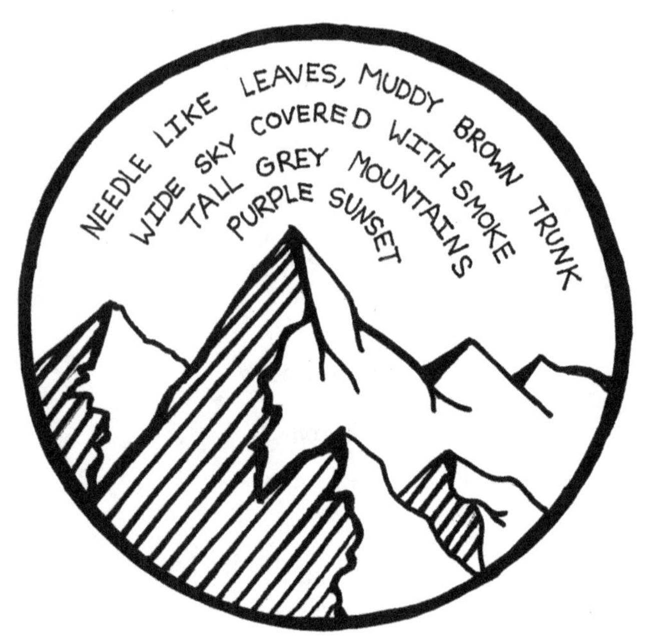

Siri Aadi Khalsa

Needle like leaves, muddy brown trunk
Wide sky covered with smoke
Tall grey mountains
Purple sunset

Oh the big puppet

Oh the big nose,

Oh the big flame that's invincible to a hose

Burn it,

eat the ashes and light the wicks.

Say goodbye to gloom, and Marilyn Monroe's fits.

Vincent Martinez

Santa Fe

Oh the big puppet
Oh the big nose,
Oh the big flame that's invincible to a hose
Burn it, eat the ashes and light the wicks.
Say goodbye to gloom, and Marilyn Monroe's fits.

*(In Santa Fe there is a tradition known as The Burning Of Zozobra.
Each year participants across the town help build and put together
a giant 50ft puppet known as Old Man Gloom or Zozobra. In
2014-Present a New Mexico man planned to put some of Marylin
Monroe's old dresses in the puppet to burn them. He stated he felt it
would be best, he disliked the idea of selling them to people.)*

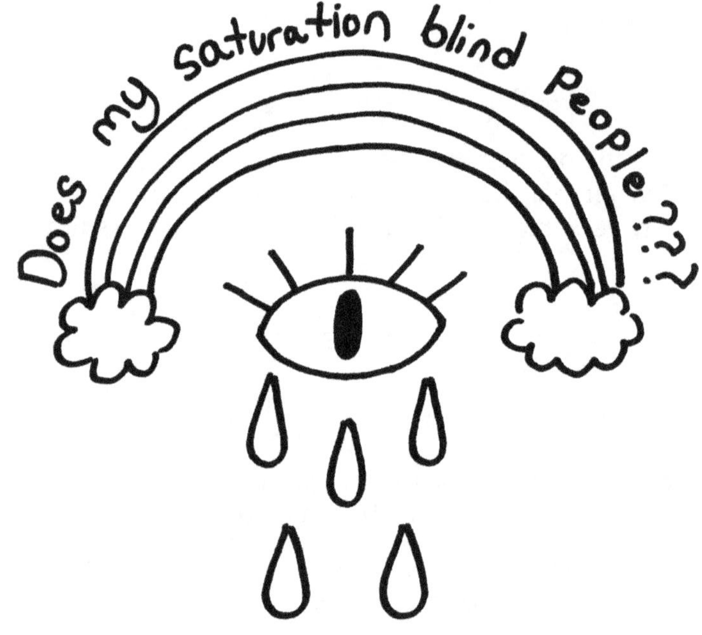

Desiree Lopez

Eye Bleeding Rainbow

My room is a colorful mess
And no one dares to enter it
No one should enter my vibrant daydream
Does my saturation blind people?
I'm happy with my eye bleeding neon colors
It'll knock the daylights out of them
And all they'll see is radiant stars
I'm not ashamed of being bright
If it hurts their sights then that's ok
Not everyone likes glaring hues
I want to push my limit
I want to stand out and really pop
It'll really burn people's orbs
But I am loved by rainbows
And that's what matters

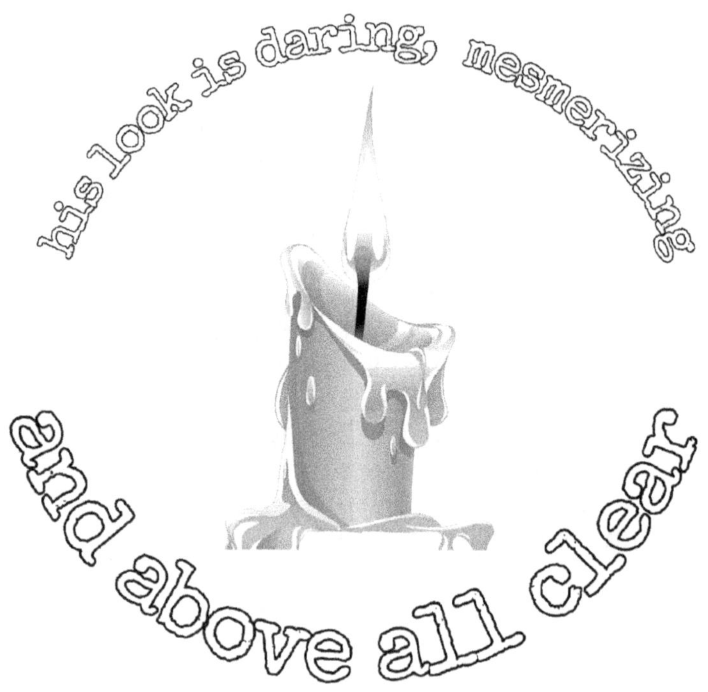

Enivid Ruiz

One Simply Lit Candle

He's a simple flame,
With simple flair.
A touch so soft,
But harmful.

He sits alone on the
Corner of a desk.
Only surrounded by
Small objects.

His look is daring,
Mesmerizing,
And above all clear.

He has no shadow,
And no true friends.

He has one simple task,
Until his life ends.
To light the world,
To light my desk.

His simple task is gone,
And I'm all alone.

For he was nothing,
But a simply lit candle.

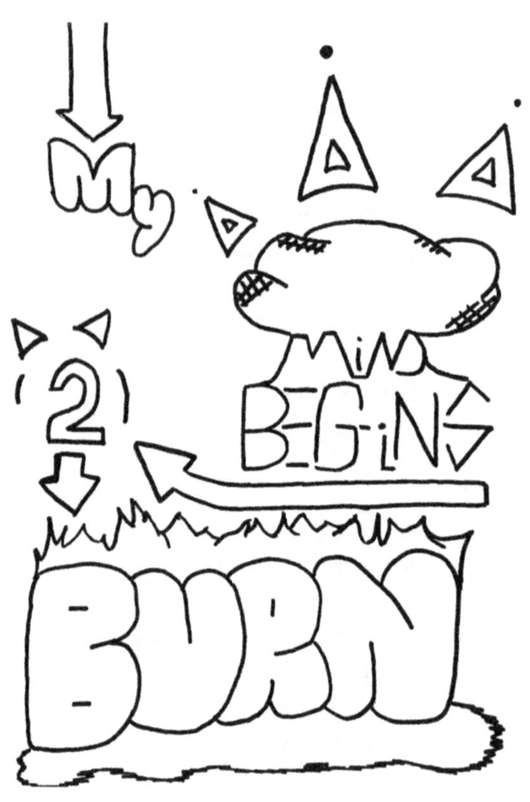

Fernando Pizano

Stale Life

The sun
    glistens

               as it rises

      To a new day

Full of hope

       and surprises
Wandering
            through the streets

              Something new in every turn
My imagination

        begins to
        burn

           Slowly about

      I go around

             To once again

return

The Shoebox

What are the things
that keep you going?
Are they

Are they   people,

         objects,
Are they

              memories,
Are they
         thoughts?
Do they stay on your
Body,
Are they a distant
              Grasp,
What presence do they
    Hold?

God,
   I've never said this
              before.

Macy Loy

The Shoebox

What are the things that keep you going?

Are they people, are they objects, are they memories,

are they thoughts?

Do they stay on your body, are they a distant grasp,

what presence do they hold?

God, I've never said this before.

In my room, under my bed, is a shoebox.

Of all the things in my life that keep me going, truthfully, this shoebox

is the one. Each letter I receive, whether valued or not, I keep. I then

place these letters in this shoebox- to hold for the rest of my time.

I have letters from my first-grade class who wrote to me

when my dog died. "We miss you in class these days..."

I have letters from every holiday I spent waking up to myself.

"This gift seemed like a cool project, wishing I could spend your

birthday with you..."

I have acceptance letters from programs I've done, declined letters from

programs I've dreamed of. "Congratulations..."

I have letters from friends now gone, people now memories.

"I wish it didn't have to be like this, I wish I didn't have to leave..."

These letters are a symbol of growth.

These letters are my values.

These letters are my core.

The shoebox under my bed is my being.

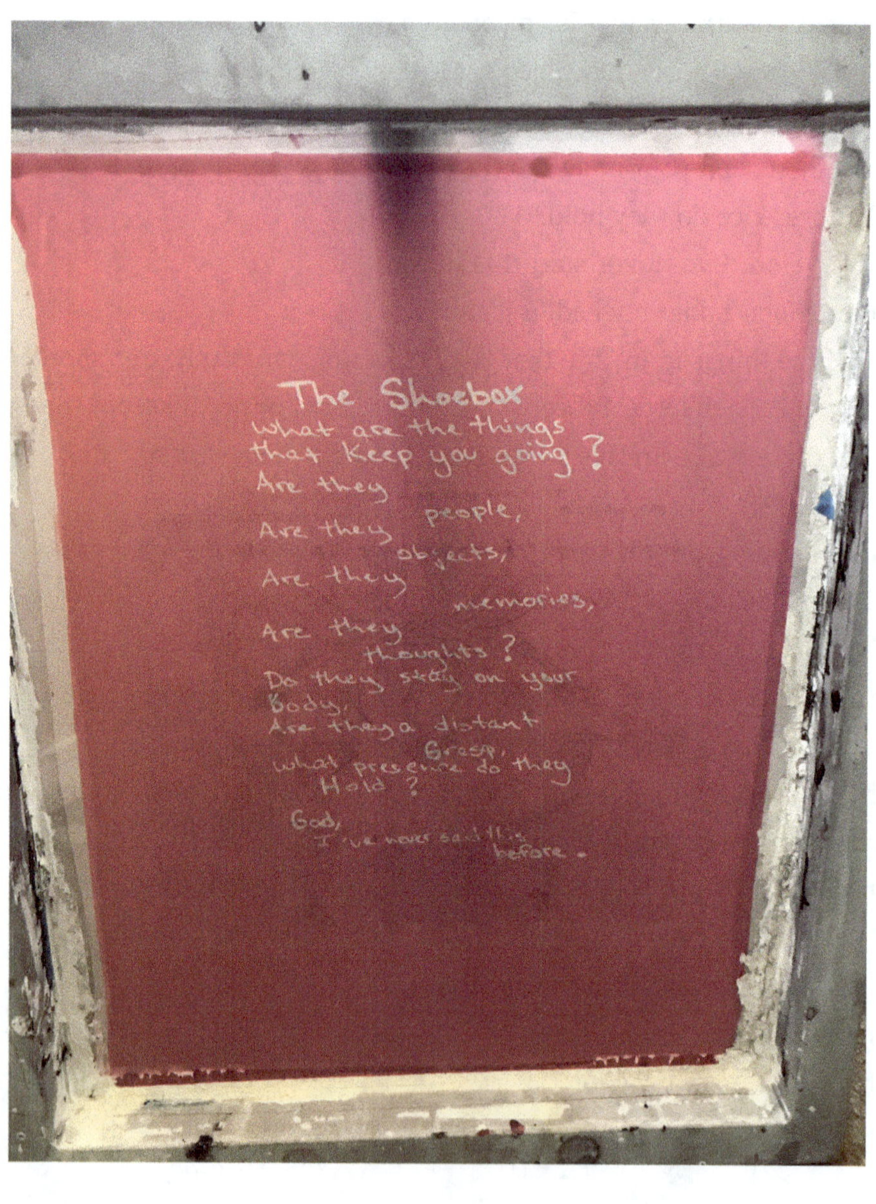
The Shoebox
What are the things
that Keep you going?
Are they
Are they   people,
            objects,
Are they
            memories,
Are they
        thoughts?
Do they stay on your
Body,
Are they a distant
            Grasp,
what pressure do they
    Hold?

God,
    I've never said this
            before.

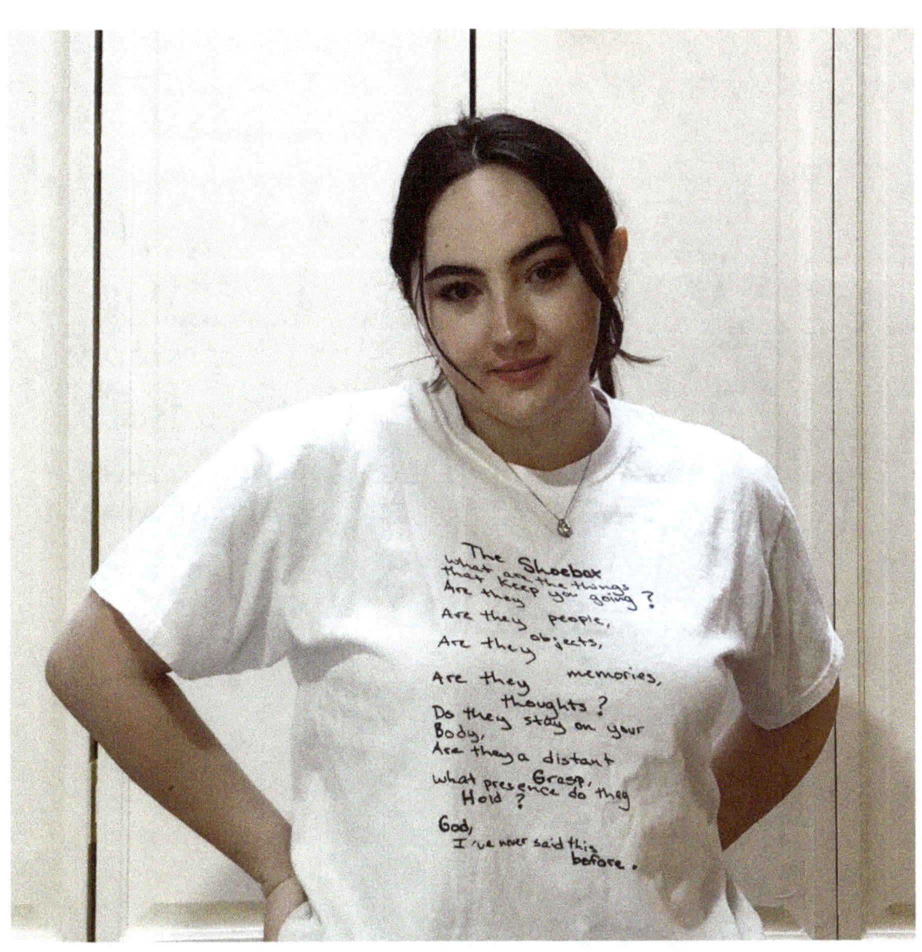

The Shoebox
What are the things
that keep you going?
Are they people,
Are they objects,
Are they memories,
thoughts?
Do they stay on your
Body,
Are they a distant
Grasp,
What presence do they
Hold?
God,
I've never said this
before.

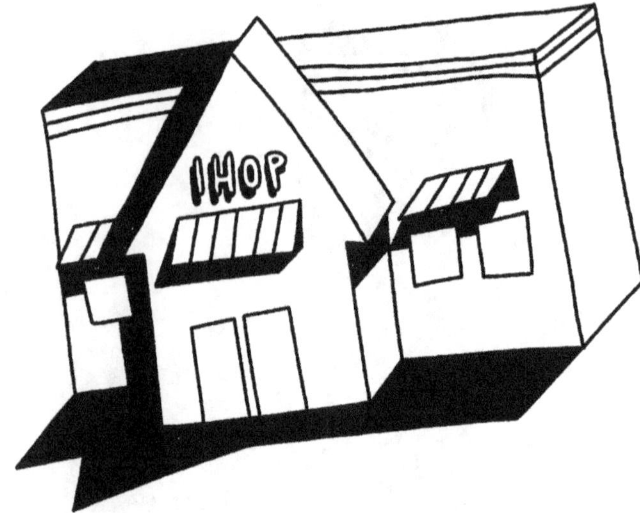

Madeleine Ingram

palisades

This place is dirty
in the same way
all of those
family restaurants are.

I'll never go back.

STAR LIGHT, STAR BRIGHT

i woke up to a

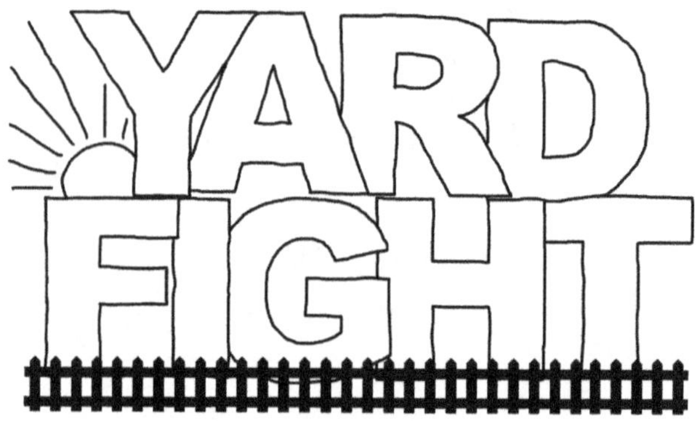

Zane Demmon

Broken Stop Lights

Star light, star bright,
I woke up to a yard fight.

It's not called night
Here, on the dark side.

              Archived.
A   Hole   in   ONE
On the par five,

            and an E tank on a long drive.

It's hard to keep wishin' with no wells to drop dimes.

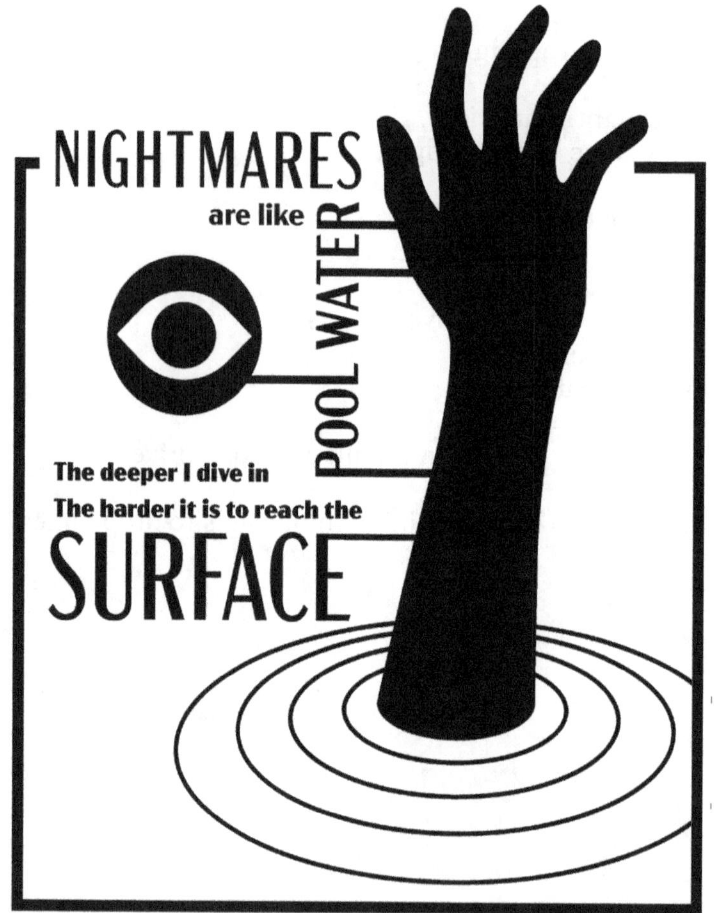

Samuel Johnston

Chlorine Dreams

Nightmares are like pool water
The more I swim
The less my eyes burn

Water stained with blue blood
Can't call for help without any proof

Ankles cut open by the shoes I wear
Some wounds leave unforgivable marks

Mutilated footsteps hidden behind curtains
Hung by the blind eye of those who think they understand

Fragile breathing behind locked doors
How can I trust the reliably unreliable

Facing fears with closed eyes
Sheltered by the still air of darkness

Nightmares are like pool water
The deeper I dive in
The harder it is to reach the surface

chokecherry pits littered
the yard

Veronica Silva

[Birdsong in july]

Flecks of mold had littered the walls like chokecherry pits in the yard
                                        for   far   too   long

I scraped my knuckles on the adobe wall,

            dirt and rocks hid in the soles of our shoes

        I was impatient,   foolish

Foolish enough to stumble once again over what I thought was
innocence
                    Did you dread leaving or staying more?

        - .... / ... - --- .-. -.-- / -. . ...- . .-. /
            . -. -.. . -.. / .-- .. - .... / -.-- --- ..-

        homesick for a place that doesn't exist

            There was always a tension between your bone and flesh

    but   the   birds   could   tell

                    they flock around tension, they can read me,
                    they taunt me.

Ice cold,   Ice cold,   I   want   to   go
                    inside   again

        The walls of your room cry to me in the night

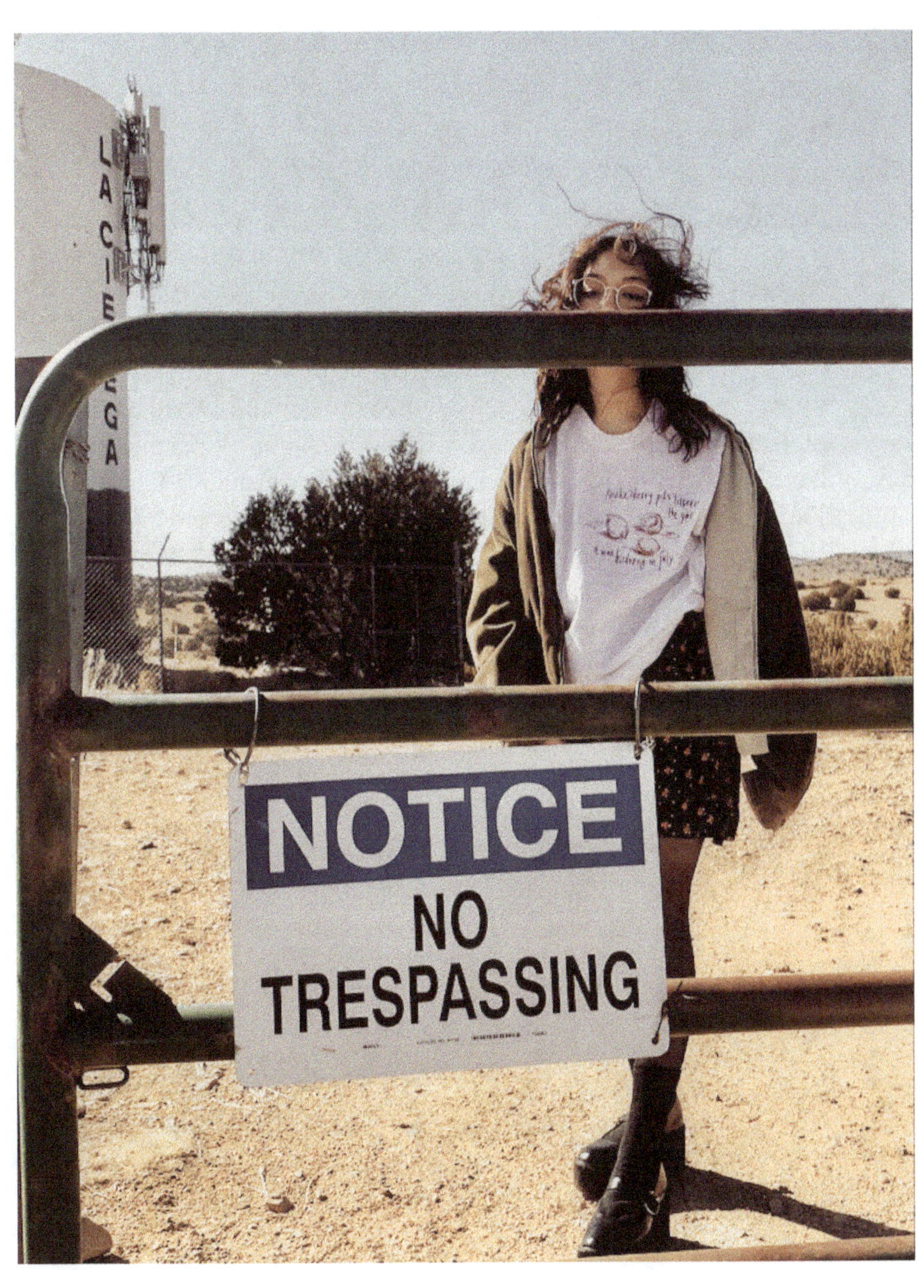

LA CIE EGA
NOTICE
NO
TRESPASSING

Acknowledgements

Boundless gratitude to everyone who supported this civic project, especially Karina Hean, James Reich and Diego Gomez at the New Mexico School for the Arts, and to all the students we worked with in Santa Fe. Melynn Schuyler and David Sloan of YouthWorks have been exceptional community partners as have Elise and Eric Gent from Railyard Performance Center; Dorothy Massey and Cecile Lipworth at Collected Works Bookstore; the City of Santa Fe Arts and Culture Department, thank you all so much. David Kaufman and DB, many, many thanks to both of you. Continuous gratitude to the Academy of American Poets for their support of this project and for all they do for poetry in the world.

Index